ity

A

MANUEL GÁLVEZ

by Myron I. Lichtblau

This book introduces the general reader to one of the most important Argentine novelists of the twentieth century. Manuel Gálvez (1882-1962) played a highly significant role in the development of Argentine fiction from 1914 to about 1945 with a long list of novels revealing the social, political, and psychological fabric of his country. Gálvez was the prolific, controversial author of some twenty-nine works of fiction portraying almost every facet of Argentine life from the provinces of La Rioja and Cordoba to hustling cosmopolitan Buenos Aires. The study provides a comprehensive view of Gálvez' fiction in addition to a detailed analysis of his major novels. Gálvez is seen as an intensely realistic novelist with deep psychological penetration into character and environmental forces. In his most important novels his characters vainly struggle against their hostile surroundings seeking social justice and reform. Gálvez used the historical novel to voice his personal beliefs and political ideology, clearly seen in his trilogy on the Paraguayan War and in the series on the dictator Rosas; and his ardent defense of Catholicism is a *leitmotiv* running through many of his best works.

TWAYNE'S WORLD AUTHORS SERIES (TWAS)

The purpose of TWAS is to survey the major writers—novelists, dramatists, historians, poets, philosophers, and critics—of the nations of the world. Among the national literatures covered are those of Australia, Canada, China, Eastern Europe, France, Germany, Greece, Italy, Japan, Latin America, the Netherlands, New Zealand, Poland, Russia, Scandinavia, Spain, and the African nations, as well as Hebrew, Yiddish, and Latin Classical literature. This survey is complemented by Twayne's United States Authors Series and English Authors Series.

The intent of each volume in these series is to present a critical-analytical study of the works of the writer; to include biographical and historical material that may be necessary for understanding, appreciation, and critical appraisal of the writer; and to present all material in clear, concise English—but not to vitiate the scholarly content of the work by doing so.

Manuel Gálvez

MANUEL GÁLVEZ

In loving memory of
my mother (1891–1968),
who inspired me to
seek knowledge.

ABOUT THE AUTHOR

Myron I. Lichtblau received his M.A. from the Universidad Nacional de Mexico and his Ph.D. from Columbia University. He is at present Professor of Latin-American Literature at Syracuse University and Chairman of the Department of Romance Languages. His special field of interest is Argentine literature, particularly contemporary fiction. Among Professor Lichtblau's books are *The Argentine Novel in the Nineteenth Century, El arte estilístico de Eduardo Mallea,* and an edition of *Las dos vidas del pobre Napoleón,* a novel by Gálvez. Some twenty articles on the Argentine novel appear in learned journals. Professor Lichtblau was executive secretary of the Instituto Internacional de Literatura Iberoamericana from 1959 to 1963, and since 1965 has been review editor of *Symposium.*

k in the development of ms from the vitality and om the formative years of he successive, although at ts through which all en in the evolution of the l Gálvez is one of the most ovel because of his realistic e life. He was the first well as one of the few this century. Unlike most ᴖeir livelihood from sources ᴖᴗᴦᴇ, Gálvez devoted himself almost exclusively to ᴖᴗ profession and was able to live from his pen. Methodical and thorough in his routine of putting ink to paper four hours each morning, he published regularly and prolifically: twenty-nine novels, two volumes of short stories, nine biographies, three dramas, three volumes of poetry, nine of essays, and four of memoirs. But although his fiction spans forty-eight years, from 1914 to 1962, his most significant and lasting novels were written in the first half of his career. Literary and commercial success with his early works propelled Gálvez into the forefront of Argentine letters. European critics, especially from Spain and France, frequently commented on his works and praised his faithful depiction of the Argentine scene. Translations of his novels in French, English, German, Italian, and even lesser-known languages such as Bulgarian and Czech, disseminated his name and helped the foreign reader gain some awareness of Latin-American fiction.

Gálvez is neither a "popular" novelist in the somewhat pejorative sense of the term nor an intellectual novelist writing for a literary élite. That the public responded so favorably to many of his early novels in no way implies a surrender to sensationalism, melodrama, or luridness.

Quite simply, his novels appealed to the reader because they were unmistakably Argentine, completely national. Gálvez was the first to write a series of novels with which Argentines could readily identify themselves and which artistically presented vital elements in their country's pattern of life. Even though his fiction treats serious social and psychological conflicts, he is rarely heavy or complex in narrative presentation and style. He shuns all literary artifice and adornment, all symbolism and involved imagery, all verbal gymnastics and structural and chronological intricacies. Gálvez' art may be too simple and direct to satisfy entirely those who seek a more involved intellectual experience. Aesthetically, he may disappoint some sophisticated readers who equate stark directness of expression with shallowness of thought, and clarity and neatness of sentence with stylistic immaturity and commonplaceness. If Gálvez' novels fail to stir the depths of our intellect, they do succeed in moving us emotionally and creating a convincing picture of Argentine society.

Although varied in subject matter and theme, Gálvez' works show a marked uniformity in novelistic technique and style. The types of fiction that predominate are the social novels of Buenos Aires and the interior provinces, historical novels on nineteenth-century Argentina, and novels with strong moralistic or religious overtones. It is within this general framework that Gálvez is presented in this book. The particular chapter divisions I have used bring out best the salient characteristics of Gálvez' art and his significance in Argentine literature. Strict adherence to chronology or theme has at times been sacrificed to achieve the most effective presentation of the novelist's works. My objective has been to combine the virtues of a limited study of a few selected novels with an overall view of Gálvez' fiction. I did not wish to contemplate the whole forest without seeing the individual trees. Some of his novels merit extensive treatment; others a briefer and less detailed examination. Still others, in particular those forming part of a series of historical novels, can best be studied as a group. To understand Gálvez the novelist, we need to know Gálvez the man, his formative years, his professional struggles, his ideas and ideals, his conduct with people, and above all his relationship to the literary environment that surrounded him. For this reason, the first chapter tries to do more than merely record the notable events in his life; its aim is to fuse the man and the writer into a cohesive unit.

The critical bibliography on Gálvez is vast, although no complete, comprehensive book on the novelist has been written prior to this study. Three short monographs and two unpublished doctoral dissertations are necessarily limited in scope. Hundreds of articles, reviews, and short commentaries study selected novels and particular aspects of his work, or deal with his political and social ideology. It is my hope, therefore, that this book will serve the general public as a guide to the understanding and appreciation of an important figure in Latin-American fiction. Appearing as it does some nine years after Gálvez' death, it enjoys the temporal perspective that is desired for a balanced evaluation.

Page numbers in the body of the text refer to the particular edition of the work I have used. Only when this is not the first edition, and therefore not listed fully in the end bibliography, have I cited it in "Notes and References."

The translations are my own except those taken from Eduardo Mallea's *La bahía de silencio* and from Gálvez' *Miércoles Santo* and *Nacha Regules.* I would like to thank Alfred A. Knopf, Inc., New York, for permission to quote from *The Bay of Silence,* translated by Stuart E. Grummon, 1944; copyright 1944 by Alfred A. Knopf, Inc. I also wish to thank John Lane The Bodley Head, Ltd., London, for permitting me to quote from *Holy Wednesday,* translated by Warre B. Wells, 1934; and Hawthorne Books, Inc., New York, which has the American and Canadian rights. In addition, I am grateful to E. P. Dutton & Co., Inc., New York, for permission to quote from the book *Nacha Regules,* translated by Leo Angley; copyright 1923 by E. P. Dutton & Co., Inc.; renewal translation copyright 1950 by E. P. Dutton & Co., Inc.; reprinted by permission of the publishers.

Some of the comments in Chapter 9 on *Las dos vidas del pobre Napoleón* appeared in another form in my introduction to a college edition of the novel, published by Charles Scribner's Sons, New York, 1963. I am greatly indebted to Scribner's for granting me permission to use this material.

With much pleasure I acknowledge my gratitude to Manuel Gálvez, who was kind enough to grant me an interview in Buenos Aires some nineteen years ago and who wrote freely about himself and his works in subsequent correspondence with me. I am deeply grateful also to the novelist's widow, María Elena Gaviola de Gálvez for her invaluable aid. Her kindness in sending me countless documents, articles, and letters relating to her husband's career, as well as several unedited stories and essays, is warmly appreciated. I owe an expression of thanks to Professors Daniel P. Testa and Jaime Ferrán of Syracuse University for offering their help on several occasions. Sincere appreciation is extended to Professors Walter Sutton and Lino Novás-Calvo, also of

Syracuse, who carefully read the entire manuscript and were kind enough to make valuable suggestions. To Professor John P. Dyson, editor of the Twayne Latin-American Authors Series, I express a deep sense of gratitude for his kindness in guiding and assisting me in the preparation of this work. For her encouragement in the planning and execution of this study, I wish to thank Professor Sylvia E. Bowman, general editor of the Twayne World Authors Series. Lastly, a word of thanks to my wife Bernice for her patience and understanding.

Syracuse University
December, 1970

MYRON I. LICHTBLAU

Contents

Chronology

1882   July 18: Born in the provincial city of Paraná, Argentina.

1883   Family moves to Santa Fe, Argentina.

1897   Graduates from a Franciscan secondary school in Buenos Aires.

1903   Founds, with Ricardo Olivera, the magazine *Ideas.*

1903–   Serves as law clerk in a criminal court in Buenos Aires.
1905

1904   Receives his law degree from the University of Buenos Aires.

1905   First trip to Europe.

1906–   Serves as Inspector of Secondary and Normal Schools.
1931

1907   With great ardor, renews religious faith he renounced in 1904. First book appears, *El enigma interior,* a volume of poetry.

1910   Marries Delfina Bunge, a writer. Second trip abroad. In Paris, as Argentine delegate to the International Conference on Unemployment. Publishes his first book revealing his philosophical and political creed, *El diario de Gabriel Quiroga.*

1912   Joins the staff of *Nosotros,* prestigious Argentine literary journal.

1913   *El solar de la raza,* volume of essays on Spain, his first commercial success.

1914   Publishes his first novel, *La maestra normal.*

1916   Publishes *El mal metafísico.*

1917   *La sombra del convento* appears. Founds the Cooperativa Editorial Buenos Aires.

1919   Founds, with Augusto Bunge, Editorial Pax. Publishes *Nacha Regules.*

1920   Founds the publishing house Biblioteca de Novelistas Americanos.

1922   *Historia de arrabal,* short naturalistic novel. *La tragedia de un hombre fuerte.*

1925 Third trip abroad. Visits Europe, Africa, and the Middle East.

1928– Three historical novels of the series *Escenas de la Guerra del*
1929 *Paraguay.*

1928– Writes twenty-five articles for the liberal Catholic magazine
1937 *Criterio.*

1930 Founds the Argentine chapter of the P.E.N. Club.

1931 Is instrumental in the establishment of the Argentine Academy of Letters and becomes one of its members. Publishes *El gaucho de Los Cerrillos,* first historical novel in the series on the Rosas era.

1932 Candidate for Nobel Prize. Also nominated in 1933 and 1951.

1938 *Hombres en soledad.*

1939 *Vida de Hipólito Yrigoyen,* biography.

1940 *Vida de don Juan Manuel de Rosas,* controversial biography.

1943– Contributes over forty articles to the Catholic newspaper *El*
1945 *Pueblo.*

1944 *Amigos y maestros de mi juventud,* first volume of memoirs.

1945 *Vida de Sarmiento,* biography of the great Argentine statesman.

1948 Resumes novel writing after a lapse of ten years with *La ciudad pintada de rojo.*

1952 Delfina Bunge de Gálvez dies.

1954 Marries María Elena Gaviola Salas. *Las dos vidas del pobre Napoleón,* whimsical novel breaking with Gálvez' strong line of realism. *Y así cayó don Juan Manuel,* last of six Rosas novels.

1956 *Tránsito Guzmán,* novel attacking Perón regime.

1961– Three remaining volumes of memoirs appear under the general
1965 title *Recuerdos de la vida literaria.*

1962 November 14: Dies in Buenos Aires at the age of eighty.

CHAPTER I

A Novelist's Life: Passion for Literature

THE story of Manuel Gálvez' life,[1] to a larger degree than that of most of his contemporaries, reveals a man for whom writing was an obsessive passion. Gálvez lived his life through his literature. His inordinate preoccupation with his work never abated during his long career. His concern over the impact of his writings on both the critics and the general public went beyond mere professional pride and dedication. His was an indomitable ego, driving him on to seek the fullest measure of recognition. Although reserved and even introverted in direct personal contacts, Gálvez delighted in the central position he held in the flourishing literary world of Buenos Aires in the early decades of this century. And in the later years of his career, when he lost ground as a literary force, he liked to think of himself as the patriarch of Argentine fiction, observing the new trends in novel writing that were taking hold in his country but disassociating himself completely from them.

I Family Background and Youthful Years

With the advantages of family position and economic security, Gálvez was able to spend a comfortable youth in intellectual and cultural pursuits, vicariously experiencing life through wide reading. He was born on July 18, 1882 in the city of Paraná, a small provincial capital 225 miles northwest of Buenos Aires. His forebears came to Argentina in early colonial times and include Juan de Garay, who founded the city of Santa Fe in 1573 and shortly thereafter refounded the original settlement of Buenos Aires. Other figures in Gálvez' lineage are Gabriel de Quiroga and Julián de Gálvez, both high-ranking officials of the Inquisition in Santa Fe. In the second half of the nineteenth century, two other Gálvezes played important roles in Sante Fe: an uncle, Dr. José Gálvez, one-time governor of the province and national senator; and the novelist's father, Dr. Manuel Gálvez, who also held several political posts, among them secretary of the treasury and national congressman.

Gálvez spent an uneventful childhood and adolescence in a traditionally religious and conservative home. His education, classical in content and scholastic in approach, was that given to most children of the upper middle class in Argentina during the closing years of the past century. When he was three years of age, the Gálvez family moved to Santa Fe, where Manuel received his primary and part of his secondary education at the Jesuit school La Inmaculada. In 1897, he completed his secondary studies in Buenos Aires at the Franciscan Colegio del Salvador. Since there were but few choices for a professional career at that time in Latin America, he reluctantly entered the Law School of the University of Buenos Aires and received his degree in 1904. It is not surprising that he never practiced his profession, for his real interest was in the humanities, particularly literature and the fine arts. For his doctoral dissertation, Gálvez wisely chose a theme which both satisfied the Law School requirements and enabled him to display his literary talents. His subject, white slavery, is evidence of his early interest in social problems that led him to write such novels as *El mal metafísico* (*The Metaphysical Ill*) and *Nacha Regules*.

Gálvez was an ingenuous and sensitive youth, quite impressionable, and with strong likes and dislikes. Diligent and intellectually curious, especially about history and social philosophy, he was the perpetual student in pursuit of culture and knowledge of the world about him. His great passion was literature; his favorite authors Dostoevski, Tolstoi, Flaubert, Zola, Pérez Galdós, Eça de Queiroz. He read extensively in the theater and was especially well versed in Spanish drama of the Golden Age and the Romantic period. For their social content, uncompromising realism, and psychological penetration, the plays of Henrik Ibsen particularly caught his attention. Yet his enthusiasm for reading did not preclude interest in more leisurely pursuits. He fenced and did gymnastics; he took private lessons in French and German and was his own tutor in English; he studied piano and music theory; and even attended a business school to master shorthand.

II *Literary Vocation and Religious Faith*

From devouring literature to creating his own was a natural step for Gálvez. The particular genre, however, that suited his talents best was more difficult to recognize. His vocation as novelist was not sharply etched in his mind until the age of thirty, when he began to write *La*

Maestra Normal (*The Normal School Teacher*). Meanwhile, with youthful confidence, he tried his hand at other literary forms—drama, poetry, and criticism. By the age of eighteen, he had written several plays,[2] none of which was ever staged or published and which he preferred to forget as unworthy adolescent pieces. Years later, looking back on his career and recognizing his limitations as a playwright, Gálvez remarked: "Here is my grave error and my misfortune. I should not have done anything else but write novels. I betrayed my vocation, I betrayed my duty."[3] But he persisted and in 1900 wrote *La conjuración de Maza* (*The Conspiracy of Maza*), a tragedy dealing with the Argentine dictator Juan Manuel de Rosas. This drama was freely converted into a *zarzuela,* a kind of musical comedy, and performed five times by the Spanish troupe Rivadavia. Although of slight importance in Gálvez' career, it was the first of many works—historical novels, biographies, and essays—to treat the controversial Rosas era. Also in 1900 he published his first work, an article on Ibsen's theater appearing in the April 15 issue of *La Nueva Epoca,* a Santa Fe newspaper founded by his uncle José. Responsible in part for this early effort at literary criticism was his mother's cousin, Floriano Zapata, who dabbled in journalism and literature and was the only one of Gálvez' family with a penchant for writing.

In Buenos Aires Gálvez mingled with other young writers who were also soon to become important literary figures: Ricardo Rojas, Emilio Becher, Alberto Gerchunoff, Carlos Alberto Leumann, Mario Bravo. He frequented the cafés, participated in spirited discussions on literature and the arts. Politically, he fancied himself as somewhat of a rebel, even espousing a form of anarchism, but without any real conviction. A vague idealism and exalted sense of social justice also characterized Gálvez and those of his literary coterie. A frequent topic of conversation was Tolstoy's Christian socialism, which Gálvez vigorously defended for its humanitarian and ethical values. And with equal fervor he attacked those who thwarted social justice: the wealthy, the upper class, the oligarchy, the hypocritical and corrupt politicians, the callous landowners, the exploiters of the masses. From his youthful spirit of rebellion stemmed his loss of religious faith in 1904. It was an impulsive and hasty decision, one that is indeed difficult to reconcile with his inherently spiritual nature except by considering it an immature act to demonstrate the magnitude of his discontent with society. It is not surprising, therefore, that his infidelity was short-lived. In 1907, he returned to his faith with rekindled ardor and dedicated the verses of *El sendero de humildad* (*The Path of Humility*) to his religious rebirth. In future novels Gálvez became a fervent defender of Catholicism, a stern moralist who not only rewarded those characters who led a devout life, but who felt that fulfillment and happiness were more readily achieved through spiritual devotion. In such works as *Miércoles Santo* (*Holy Wednesday*), 1930, and *La noche toca a su fin* (*Night Draws to a Close*), 1935, he probed the spiritual essence of man as a Catholic novelist, while in other works such as *El cántico espiritual* (*The Spiritual Hymn*), 1923, his religious faith hovered over the destiny of the characters or at least made itself felt in their actions and thoughts.

III *Writing for Literary Journals*

Convinced that the young intellectuals of his generation needed a literary organ, Gálvez founded in 1903, together with Ricardo Olivera, the magazine *Ideas*. Because of financial difficulties it ceased publication after only two years, but not before it served Gálvez well as a school of literary apprenticeship, affording him intellectual discipline and firm habits of concentrated work as a writer and editor.[4] Juan Pablo Echagüe handled national literature, Emilio Becher French literature, while Ricardo Rojas, who was to become his country's foremost critic, was in charge of both Spanish and Latin-American letters. Gálvez chose the world theater as his particular domain in *Ideas,* but also wrote on contemporary Argentine literature. The reviews and articles he penned[5] did not entirely please even the young Gálvez, but what did afford him much personal satisfaction was his column entitled "Chronicles of the Month," perhaps because it gave him an opportunity to express his liberal views on Argentine society. These chronicles, he states, revealed his "fervent revolutionary bent and a very aggressive spirit." [6] The magazine achieved its greatest commercial success with an issue containing an article in French entitled "La jeune fille d'aujourd'hui, est-elle heureuse?" The author of the article was Delfina Bunge, a talented young woman who in 1910 became Gálvez' wife. Although ingenuous and at times sentimentally idealistic, the article afforded interesting psychological insights into aristocratic society. This issue attracted a wider public than any other one and was sold out within a few days.

Gálvez' brief but rewarding experience with *Ideas* was the first of many associations with literary and cultural publications. In 1912 he joined the staff of *Nosotros,* a much more notable and stable journal, and was soon put in charge of the fine arts section. During his three years with *Nosotros,* he developed into an accomplished art critic, writing articles such as "The National Exposition of Fine Arts" (November, 1912) and "The Third Exposition of Belgian Art" (April, 1913). Although not formally trained in art, his natural aesthetic sensitivity, refined by self-study and long hours in the famous museums of Europe, enabled him to write with ease and assurance on both classical and modern painting and sculpture. Beauty of form, harmony of expression, and classical simplicity dominate his artistic values in much the same way that simple naturalness characterizes his narrative art. From 1912 to 1914, at about the same time he wrote for *Nosotros,* he also edited the Argentine literature section of the *Revista de América,* which Francisco García Calderón published in Paris. Among Gálvez' writings for this journal is a review (September, 1912) of Ricardo Rojas' famous work *Blasón de plata* (*Silver Heraldry*).

Three religiously oriented magazines and one Catholic newspaper provided Gálvez with an opportunity to express his ideas on morality and the spiritual nature of man, as well as on other themes ranging from contemporary political figures to Russian literature. From 1926 to 1931, he contributed nine articles to *Ichthys,*[7] a modest journal put out by the Centro de Estudios Religiosos, which his wife Delfina directed. In the nine-year period beginning in 1928 he wrote twenty-five articles for *Criterio,*[8] whose enlightened philosophy attracted much unfavorable attention in religious circles. At the core of many of Gálvez' articles was a plea for less pomp and ritual and more genuine faith. The words of Ignacio Anzoátegui, one of the principal supporters of *Criterio,* express Gálvez' own feelings: "People thought until that moment (when the magazine appeared) that to be Catholic it was necessary to put on 'a Catholic face,' that faith was a kind of state . . . of intellectual drowsiness, and that virtue was but a form of unctuosity."[9] In 1929, seeking another forum for the liberal spirit in Catholicism, Gálvez helped found the journal *Número,* in which he published three articles.[10] And in 1943 he felt honored when the Catholic newspaper *El Pueblo* invited him to contribute articles on themes of his choice. From 1943 to 1945 he published forty-two articles in *El Pueblo,*[11] some no more than brief notes, others more substantial and more carefully prepared, all written with intense personal conviction. During these two years, he produced no novels, but was engaged in writing the biographies of Aparicio Saravia, Domingo F. Sarmiento, and José Hernández. His mind was attentive to historical questions and current national conflicts. Politics, political systems, and social problems were of more real and immediate concern to Gálvez in the 1940's than perhaps at any other period in his life.

World War II opened up the thorny question of Argentine neutrality, which he strongly supported in many articles in *El Pueblo*. For Gálvez, strained Argentine-United States relations stemmed in part from the clash between Yankee economic imperialism and the search for authentic national identity and political sovereignty.

Gálvez' fecundity and intellectual energy were amazing, for besides his sixty books he published some four hundred articles, commentaries, and reviews in the forenamed journals as well as in *Atlántida, Leoplán, Il Mattino d'Italia, El Hogar,* and others. Considering his intense devotion to fiction and biography, it is remarkable that he expended so much effort with these journalistic and incidental writings. Yet, if we look at them carefully, we see that they were far more than incidental pieces, but formed a close thematic bond with his novels and biographical works. No small part of what he said in article form he treated in fiction or biography. At times the article anticipated the novel; other times the article reinforced points of view already made evident in the novel. In either case, Gálvez divulged the same ideas in different writings, but not necessarily to the same public. Many Argentines who never read his novels or biographies became acquainted with his ideas through magazines and newspapers. His wide range of public exposure as a serious novelist, social and political commentator, literary critic, and journalist has few parallels in Argentine letters.

IV *Sentimental Verses*

A volume of poetry, *El enigma interior* (*The Inner Enigma*), 1907, was Gálvez' first published book. Youthful, melancholy verses, they were written, as the author succinctly put it, because he was in love. The thoughts expressed were trite and naïvely idealistic; the tone sad and at times anguished; the mood romantically somber. They were verses of young Gálvez' disillusion with his material surroundings, of his confused sensations in a world he did not quite understand. He made no pretense of possessing unusual poetic talent, although when he claimed Heinrich Heine and Paul Verlaine as his masters it was seemingly with a touch of regret that his gift for poetry was not greater. In 1909, Gálvez came out with *El sendero de humildad,* a better volume of verses than *El enigma interior,* but still lacking in poetic artistry. The *modernista* movement was at its height, with its cult of beauty and art for art's sake, with its escape from reality and its refuge in an ivory tower of things artificial and distant, of princesses and marquesses, of Nordic gods and ancient Greece, of swans and pheasants. An artistic temperament more remote from these things than Gálvez' could hardly be found. While rejecting the aesthetic principles and themes of Modernist poetry, he recognized the musicality and rhythm of its verses. More than anything else, *El sendero de humildad* was his negative reaction to *modernismo* and an affirmation of his creed of naturalness and spontaneity in literary expression. The themes that attracted him the most in these early verses include the simple daily experiences of the people of the Argentine provinces. His verses speak of childhood reminiscences, of placid town squares, of organ grinders, of old houses, of poor folk, of the joys of country living. The sentiments expressed are those of humility and goodness, and above all renewed religious faith. The plain, unornamented language accords well with these simple themes; yet all too frequently this simplicity and directness of style are flatly prosaic and lack artistic sensibility. Although *El sendero de humildad* is today hardly remembered, it anticipates two essential traits of the novelist-to-be: realistic presentation of environment and an unusually natural and lucid style. Gálvez' muse was silent for some forty-five years during his long career as a novelist and biographer. Then in 1954, on the occasion of his second marriage to María Elena Gaviola de Salas, he published *Poemas para la recién llegada* (*Poems for the Newcomer*) as an expression of love for the woman who was to be his companion until his death some eight years later. It is the sentimental poetry of an aging man who feels grateful for the solace his much younger wife gives him. The verses are more mature and restrained than in his two previous volumes, but are just as undistinguished.

V *Essays and Ideas*

In his lifetime Gálvez held only two remunerative positions not directly related to his literary career. From 1903 to 1905, when he worked so arduously on *Ideas,* he also served as law clerk in a criminal and correctional court in the Argentine capital. This modest post frequently placed him in close contact with the wretched living conditions of the lower classes and aroused his interest in social reform. Far more important was his appointment in 1906 as Inspector of Secondary and Normal Schools, a position he held for twenty-five years. His duties apparently made few demands on his time or energy, for during this period he wrote some eighteen books, including many of his best novels. During the first years of office, his semiannual inspection tours of schools in central and northern Argentina enabled him to gain the first-hand knowledge of provincial life that he drew on in his early novels *La maestra normal* and *La sombra del convento* (*The Shadow of the Convent*).

With a disciplined restraint that ran through most of his life, Gálvez deferred the writing of novels until he was thirty, when he felt he would possess the intellectual and literary maturity, as well as worldly experience, that fiction requires. But, as already noted, until that time his pen was active in other literary genres. In 1910 he put out a volume of personal essays entitled *El diario de Gabriel Quiroga* (*The Diary of Gabriel Quiroga*), in which he expounded, often contentiously, on many subjects that have long divided Argentines and that recur later in his novels and biographies: federalism versus unitarianism, the role of the Catholic church, the greatness of Sarmiento, immigration, the dynamic Buenos Aires versus the stagnant rural and provincial regions. Above all Gálvez showed himself to be an ardent Catholic who believed that the essence of the Argentine psyche was molded indelibly by the spirit of Catholicism. He was as well a zealous nationalist who refused to compromise with Argentina's sovereignty and economic independence. Passionately proud of his country's Spanish heritage, he believed that the several immigrant groups—Italian, French, and English—should become spiritually assimilated into the mainstream of Argentine life and be less concerned about material advancement. In Argentina's postindependence struggle for political stability, Gálvez had no sympathy for the Unitarian cause, which he felt was controlled by an intellectual and social élite that cared little for the lot of the common man and would have betrayed the nation's sovereignty to French and English interests. A careful reading of *El diario de Gabriel Quiroga* leaves little doubt that it contains the essence of Gálvez' social, religious, and political thought, anticipating the underlying themes of his future novels. It is his manifesto, a valuable document attesting to the inalterability of his fundamental beliefs over a span of some fifty-five years.

A trip to Europe to imbibe continental culture was expected of a promising young Latin-American writer. Gálvez departed on his quest in 1905, immediately after *Ideas* ceased publication. His itinerary was the customary one through Spain, France, Italy, and Germany. With his first book yet to appear, he was eager to widen his literary contacts and become acquainted with leading writers. In Paris he met the great Nicaraguan poet Rubén Darío; in Italy he met Marinetti; and in Madrid the Spanish writers Pardo Bazán, Valle-Inclán, and Pérez de Ayala. Side by side with his passion for literature was his deep interest in art, and he found his classroom in the Louvre, the Prado, and the Uffizi. He did more than just tour the galleries; he studied and interpreted the paintings as a serious student of art. His marriage to Delfina Bunge in 1910 provided him with intellectual stimulation and shared interests. With his bride, he again visited Paris, this time as the Argentine government's delegate to the International Conference on Unemployment. Although his official duties lasted no more than a few weeks, Gálvez stayed abroad for over a year and again traveled through Europe. Spain in particular, whose art and literature had always attracted his attention, now beckoned to him spiritually and religiously. He saw Spain through more mature eyes as the maternal spirit of the Argentine people, as its irrevocable heritage.[12] His itinerary also included Istanbul, Athens, Tunisia, and Algeria, places he recalled in many articles he wrote for *Atlántida, La Nación,* and *La Prensa.* In 1925, accompanied by Delfina, Gálvez made his third and last trip abroad, visiting Palma de Mallorca, Naples, and Rome, and stopping briefly in Athens, Jerusalem, and Cairo. Greece, especially, left a deep impression on him, so much so that on his return to Argentina the following year he began to study ancient Greek. And in the thirties he took up modern Greek on his own and acquired a sufficient reading knowledge of the language to translate contemporary short stories into Spanish.[13]

His mission to Paris in 1910 as delegate to the conference on unemployment prompted Gálvez to publish *La inseguridad de la vida obrera (The Uncertainty of the Workingman's Life),* 1913. The work is a documented treatise revealing his concern for the plight of the worker in Argentina and throughout the world. Some of the problems treated in this book, such as low wages and poor working conditions, were considered again in *Nacha Regules* and other novels. In *La inseguridad,* Gálvez was the reformer, the social idealist, the critic of the privileged classes; as a novelist he would soon earn the same appellations. The year 1913 also marks the appearance of his first prose work of literary value—*El solar de la raza (The Birthplace of Our Race).* Winner of the third National Prize in literature, it records his impressions of Spain during his 1910 sojourn. It is a beautifully written book that underscores the cultural and spiritual affinity between Argentina and the mother country. Spain continues to live in Argentina, Gálvez reiterates at every turn, and Argentina has to draw its inspiration and values from Spain. *El solar de la raza* consists of colorful essays describing the cities and regional cultures of Spain, from Salamanca to Granada, from Avila to the Basque Provinces. Acclaimed throughout the Spanish-speaking world, the work gave Gálvez his first commercial success and helped spread his fame as an important literary figure. One Argentine critic[14] pointed out that *El solar de la raza* should have convinced Gálvez that his real talents were in prose, not in poetry. The budding novelist could easily be seen in the vivid descriptions of social environment and nature that abound in these essays. No other book by Gálvez received such unanimous praise from so many distinguished Spanish writers and critics, including Miguel de Unamuno, Ricardo León, Andrés González Blanco, and Ricardo Monner Sanz. León said that *El solar de la raza* represented "one of the most ardent and moving apologies for Spain's national spirit that could be made."[15]

Although Gálvez continued to publish occasional volumes of essays throughout his career, they assumed less and less importance as he achieved recognition as a novelist. Such works as *Este pueblo necesita* (*What This Country Needs*), 1934, and *España y algunos españoles* (*Spain and a Few Spaniards*), 1945, provided a needed outlet for his ideas and opinions on many subjects, ranging from the meaning of democracy to his country's social ills, from the Spanish novelist Benito Pérez Galdós to the Argentine poet José Hernández. Gálvez' unremitting lament, that Argentine writers suffered unjustly because of an indifferent public and mercenary publishers, was echoed in *La Argentina en nuestros libros* (*Argentina in Our Books*), 1935. Books by national authors were slighted in favor of European works, the Argentine writer was not respected as in Europe, the government did little to promote literature—this was the unfortunate state of affairs that Gálvez depicted innumerable times in his novels and other writings.

VI *The Patron of Literature*

Gálvez' interest in things literary transcended his own ambition to be recognized as Argentina's most important novelist. It was an unwavering commitment to promote the cause of national literature and to divulge that literature to the outside world. It was also a desire to introduce Argentine readers to the best works of European authors, particularly the French. His lifelong struggle on behalf of literature endeared him to many authors, but also ensnared him in the web of professional discord and partisanship. In 1917, after gaining much recognition with *La maestra normal, El mal metafísico,* and *La sombra del convento,* he ventured into publishing and succeeded quite well. He founded the editorial house Cooperativa Editorial Buenos Aires and became one of the few publishers at that time promoting Argentine literature. Most publishers, he claimed, were no more than book dealers who issued three or four volumes annually on law or history. Gálvez understood how difficult it was for a creative writer to have his works published in Argentina. Only a few authors managed to have their books published in Spain or France or had the financial means to put out private editions. For Gálvez, Argentine writers deserved to have a more accessible road to publication and the establishment of the Cooperativa responded to this urgent need. As its first selection, it offered a book of verses, *Ciudad* (*City*), by Baldomero Fernández Moreno, at that time completely unknown but later recognized as one of Argentina's best poets. There followed a volume of stories by the noted Uruguayan Horacio Quiroga, after which appeared works by important Argentine writers: Arturo Capdevila's *El libro de la noche* (*The Book of the Night*), Benito Lynch's *Raquela,* and Alfonsina Storni's *Dulce daño* (*Sweet Harm*). One of Gálvez' own works, *La sombra del convento,* was published by the Cooperativa, the novelist himself paying for the edition and giving the corporation forty percent of the proceeds. Recalling many years later that one of his colleagues had accused him of selfish motives in starting the enterprise, Gálvez was quick to point out that "I did not need it to publish my books. I wanted to lend it my name and give it the chance to earn a few pesos." [16] An assiduous worker, he administered the Cooperativa practically by himself. He selected the books to be published and only on rare occasions consulted the board of directors, whose president was the modernist writer Angel de Estrada. Besides, he edited the manuscripts, made arrangements with the printer, read proof, supervised the retail distribution, and served as advertising manager. His high-handed editorial policies and the irresponsibility of some of the stockholders soon split the Cooperativa. Tension between Gálvez and the editorial board mounted, until one particular incident caused him to leave the organization in anger. The confrontation occurred in 1922, when the board, which previously had not even asserted its prerogatives, took a firm stand and decided to publish a book over Gálvez' objection. The work was *Crítica negativa* (*Negative Criticism*) by Nicolás Coronado, a captious Argentine critic. Referring to certain portions of the book that seemed to strike out against Argentine writers, Gálvez indignantly reminded the board that "the Cooperativa was founded to favor Argentine literature and not to discredit it." [17] Without his leadership, the organization lost vitality and finally ceased publication in 1926. Gálvez considered the Cooperativa a personal triumph, and to a large measure it was. He guided it and nurtured it, perhaps too authoritatively, certainly too much as a

one-man operation. Although its explicit goal was to extend its hand to
Argentine authors, it did not exclude writers from other Latin-
American countries. Besides Horacio Quiroga, other non-Argentine
authors who added prestige to the Cooperativa were the Bolivian
modernist poet Ricardo Jaimes Freyre and the Uruguayan poetess
Juana de Ibarbourou.[18]

In 1919, Gálvez founded, with Augusto Bunge, a second publishing
house, Editorial Pax. Its first book was a translation of the German war
novel *Man Is Good,* by Leonhard Frank. Its second was Gálvez' novel
Nacha Regules, which became his best-selling and most translated work.
Once again his detractors claimed he established Pax to insure the
publication of his own works, but the assertion seems unfounded.
Certainly our novelist had no reason to be so overtly opportunistic or
so apprehensive for the fate of his manuscripts. Then too, since the
expressed objective of Pax was to publish foreign works, not national
ones, he could not have been thinking of it as an outlet for his own
writings. In 1920, Gálvez founded still another editorial house, the
Biblioteca de Novelistas Americanos, which had as one of its principal
goals that of creating a literary bond among Latin-American authors.
Many outstanding works of fiction were published by the Biblioteca,
among them *Un perdido* (*Beaten by Life*) by the Chilean Eduardo
Barrios and *Este era un país* (*This Was a Country*) by the Uruguayan
Vicente A. Salaverri. Argentine works published in the Biblioteca
include Benito Lynch's gaucho novel *Los Caranchos de La Florida* (*The
Vultures of La Florida*) as well as Gálvez' first volume of short stories,
Luna de miel y otras narraciones (*Honeymoon and Other Stories*).
Unfortunately, Gálvez succumbed to the pressures of friendship and
published many books that brought neither credit to the Biblioteca nor
sufficient financial return to help sustain its operation. After its
collapse in 1923, he renounced all further publishing activities and
devoted himself more fully to writing fiction. In fact, he entered his
most prolific period as a novelist, publishing eight works from 1922 to
1932.

Yet if Gálvez never encumbered himself again with editorial
responsibilities, he did embark on other kindred ventures to abet the
cause of literature in his country. In March of 1930, the president of
the London P.E.N. Club, the novelist John Galsworthy, sent him a
personal letter urging him to establish an Argentine chapter. Honored
and pleased, he quickly responded to the request and on April 8 the
Argentine P.E.N. was officially founded. Appropriately, Gálvez became
its first president, with the poet Arturo Capdevila as treasurer and the

young novelist Eduardo Mallea as secretary. The purpose of the P.E.N. Clubs (Poets, Essayists, Novelists) is to foster an international community of writers, whereby members from one country may welcome their foreign colleagues as visitors and arrange meetings to exchange ideas and discuss literary projects. Argentine writers, many of whom felt removed from the mainstream of universal literature, enthusiastically supported the club and insured its success. A large share of the credit for P.E.N.'s achievements, especially in its first three years, must go to Gálvez.

In 1931, a year after he created the P.E.N., Gálvez proposed to the Argentine government that an Academy of Letters be founded "to dignify the writer so that, in the public's eye, his profession might enjoy the highest prestige." [19] With his leadership, support for the Academy came easily. The Minister of Public Education, Guillermo Rothe, instructed him to suggest ten names as candidates for membership in the Academy. He submitted eleven recommendations and all but two were accepted. Four more were added to the final list of elected members.[20] On September 11, 1931, the Academy was officially founded, with the poet Calixto Oyuela as president. From the start, Gálvez' association with the Academy was not a happy one. It was marked by acrimonious disputes over the initial selection of members as well as by professional jealousy and dissension. In 1933, he resigned, principally because he felt that justice had been denied him when he was not awarded the first National Prize in literature for that year.

VII   *The Nobel Prize Candidate*

Gálvez aspired to the most coveted prize in literature and almost won it. Three times, in 1932, 1933, and again in 1951, he was Latin America's candidate for the Nobel Prize. His best chance came in 1932, when he was in the forefront of Latin-American fiction and had recently published the third and last volume of the trilogy on the Paraguayan War. Most of his supporters believed that his strength as a candidate rested as much on this historical fiction as on his earlier social novels. Although by 1932 he had written all but one of his most enduring novels, he felt that his nomination for the Nobel Prize might be premature. At the age of fifty, with twenty-six works published, including fourteen novels, he would not believe that his career had already enjoyed its most successful days, but proudly nurtured the hope that greater recognition was still to come. Despite his apparent modesty in not considering himself ready for the candidacy, he affirmed with bold self-esteem that he was the best novelist to represent America if the Swedish Academy wished to grant the prize to a Latin American.[21] It is clear that Gálvez' information about the selection procedure was not quite accurate, but his assertion indicates how conscious he was of his reputation beyond Argentina's borders, of his place in the development of Latin-American fiction. Argentina's intellectual élite looked at his candidacy with divided feelings: vigorous approbation by the majority and strenuous disapproval by a significant minority. Men of letters such as Arturo Capdevila, Rafael Alberto Arrieta, Carmelo Bonet, Enrique Banchs, and Jorge Max Rhode would entertain no other candidate but Gálvez. Novelists such as Hugo Wast and Atilio Chiappori were loyal supporters of his cause. So too were Leopoldo Herrera, editor of *La Prensa,* and Juan B. Terán, one-time rector of the University of Tucumán. Ironically, the same Argentine Academy of Letters that Gálvez had helped to found refused to endorse him, although many individual members did. He would long remember this slight. He smarted too from the rebuff of several professors of literature at the University of Buenos Aires who thought that the poet Leopoldo Lugones was a more worthy candidate. Equally disappointing was the bland response of some Argentine newspapers, in particular *La Nación* and *El Mundo.* In other countries of America, in Venezuela, Colombia, Uruguay, and Chile, Gálvez received strong general support. But it was in Cuba and Brazil that he was most enthusiastically received. Thirteen members of the Cuban National Academy of Arts and Letters, including the illustrious essayist Enrique José Varona, signed a statement of support and sent it to Stockholm. Likewise, many members of the Brazilian Academy of Letters, as well as a score of writers, critics, and professors, acclaimed his candidacy. From the United States, such distinguished Hispanists as J.D.M. Ford of Harvard, Federico de Onís of Columbia, Frederik Luquiens of Yale, and Alfred Coester of Stanford vigorously supported Gálvez.[22]

He was proposed again as a Nobel candidate the following year, 1933, but with little expectation of winning. Eighteen years passed, and in 1951 he became a contender for the third time, his candidacy being the subject of bitter controversy and considerable confusion. In 1950, the Nobel Prize selection committee requested the ADEA, the Association of Argentine Writers, to propose a candidate. Its choice was Manuel Gálvez and his name was cabled to Stockholm. Then, some two weeks later, the same committee made an identical request of a rival Argentine literary organization, the SADE, the Argentine Society of Writers. This group considered four names: the novelist Enrique

Larreta, the dean of Argentine letters Ricardo Rojas, the essayist Ezequiel Martínez Estrada, and Manuel Gálvez. After much contention, the ultimate decision was left in the hands of the president of SADE, Carlos Alberto Erro. He chose Martínez Estrada, who he thought was a more deserving and stronger candidate than Gálvez. Argentina thus had two nominees for the Nobel Prize in 1951, neither of whom was successful in winning the award. With his compelling urge to be linked with the great names of world letters, Gálvez stated resignedly: "My defeat did not faze me. World renowned colleagues of mine were also defeated that year: Benedetto Croce, Pío Baroja, Menéndez Pidal, and, I believe, Paul Claudel." [23]

VIII *Along Varied Literary Paths*

Although Gálvez complained constantly about the meager re-muneration he received from his writings, it appears that he lived comfortably throughout his life. Some property left to him by his father provided a small additional income. Socially, he knew people from the highest circles, but preferred to limit his engagements to an occasional visit with close friends. His tastes were simple and after fifty he led an austere life. He never smoked or drank and prided himself on his moral and religious discipline. No doubt he enjoyed good health and domestic tranquility while he wrote so assiduously over a period of some fifty-five years. He had one physical defect, however, that affected the course of his fiction. At the age of eighteen he suffered a loss of hearing and by forty he was almost deaf. After 1922, he felt less able to write socially oriented novels, like *El mal metafísico,* because "my deafness, in isolating me from the outside world, did not allow me to keep abreast of new customs and ways of speech." [24] Only one important work written after 1922, *Hombres en soledad (Men in Solitude),* treats of man at odds with his environment. And in that novel Gálvez' deafness did not limit him, since the milieu protrayed, the intellectual and social life of Buenos Aires in the early 1900's, was already thoroughly known to him through direct personal contact. Reasons other than his deafness entered into his decision to veer from his initial and successful type of fiction. The nature of his writings from 1922 on gives the best clue. Wanting to combine fiction with his deep interest in history, he composed many historical novels: three on the Paraguayan War of 1865–1870, six on the era of the tyrant Rosas from 1829–1852, and one on the English invasions of 1805–1806. He also became a biographer, publishing nine works from 1933 to 1947. And to demonstrate his concern for the higher spiritual values of life, he wrote several novels of a religious or moral nature. It is idle to speculate, but had Gálvez written two or three more good "novels of environment" after 1922, he might have maintained his position far longer as Argentina's most important novelist.

After 1940, Gálvez' star began to dim. No longer was he in the front rank of the national novel, although his significant contribution to Argentine fiction was never questioned. From 1940 until the closing years of his life he wrote much, perhaps too much, but very little of importance in fiction. If by 1940 his creative talents were diminishing, in the field of biography he was just beginning to try his wings, and with no little success. From 1938 to 1948, he abandoned fiction and devoted himself to recreating the lives of famous men in Latin-American history and of a few not so famous. He became a professional historian who locked himself for hours in the libraries and archives of Buenos Aires, seeking detailed data and documentation to support his writings. It was a labor of love, perhaps affording him as much satisfaction as his novels. He relived Argentina's history through his biographies of Rosas, Yrigoyen, and Sarmiento, and while his sincerity and seriousness of purpose are never placed in doubt, his historical impartiality may be easily challenged. As Gálvez withdrew from fiction and took up biography, he became less a literary figure and more a skillful polemist with strong views on historical questions and contemporary issues. And he played the role well, aggressively defending his position and never giving quarter. He delighted in the attention paid to his political and moral ideology on such issues as Argentine sovereignty, dictatorship, nationalism, the Church, and United States imperialism. The reputation of Gálvez the novelist suffered as Gálvez the historiographer became more popular, although in his own mind he could not admit such a division in critical appraisal of his total work as a writer.

Inevitably, in 1948, he returned to fiction. He was then sixty-five, still driven by an insatiable need to write books and keep his career alive. He especially wanted to complete the series of novels on the Rosas era that he had begun in 1931 with *El gaucho de Los Cerrillos* (*The Gaucho of the Cerrillos*) and continued in 1932 with *El General Quiroga* (*General Quiroga*). These works drew only slight attention, but Gálvez felt that the public would be more receptive in the 1950's to subsequent novels on Rosas because of its demonstrated interest in his 1940 biography of the dictator. With this sense of false encouragement he set to work and in 1948 published the third novel in the series, *La ciudad pintada de rojo* (*The City Painted Red*). The remaining novels followed rapidly. When in 1954 the last novel appeared, *Y así cayó don Juan Manuel* (*The Fall of Don Juan Manuel*), he viewed with great pride his ambitious project started twenty-three years before. Yet he was disappointed at the public's tepid reaction to each novel and failed to understand the critics' lack of enthusiasm and even deliberate silence. The Rosas novels contributed little to Gálvez' reputation, perhaps even hurt it at a time when he needed another successful novel to shore up his career.

Neither these reverses nor his seventy-two years, however, deterred him. Without doubt spurred on by the solicitous hand of his second wife, Gálvez continued to write fiction and from 1954 to 1958 came out with four novels. They are all minor works which we shall have occasion to treat in a later chapter. Like the Rosas series, his last novels cannot match in artistic quality or novelistic interest those earlier works on which his reputation must ultimately rest. In the later years of his life, although exercising little influence over the course of Argentine fiction, he was a respected figure looked upon as the preserver of the conventional novel that the practitioners of the more experimental forms of fiction have sought to disclaim. He certainly was not forgotten, nor were his works unread. Until his death in 1962 he was sufficiently in the public eye to be the subject of scores of articles in newspapers and magazines. Numerous celebrations honoring the novelist and his works were held in Buenos Aires, and if he had lived just two more years he would have exulted over the many encomiastic pages written on the fiftieth anniversary of his first and best novel, *La maestra normal.*

CHAPTER 2

Argentina Finds its Novelist

I *A Glance Backward*

MANUEL Gálvez' significant contribution to the development of the Argentine novel is more readily grasped by considering him in relation to his predecessors and early contemporaries. He was the first novelist who artistically presented a comprehensive view of Argentine life in a manner that captured the national spirit and reflected the Argentine idiom. What legacy did the preceding seventy-five years of fiction hand down to him? Nineteenth-century fiction in Argentina failed to produce a single complete novelist of note, although there were a few who wrote many mediocre works or just one or two isolated works of merit. The years 1850 to 1900 represent the opening chapters in the Argentine novel.[1] And during this period Argentina was not unlike other Latin-American countries that ushered in fiction under the influence of literary movements imported from France, Spain, and England. Fledglings have no recourse but to follow a path already charted for them. In technique and aesthetic concept, the nineteenth century was imitative or at least derivative. In Argentina, romanticism thrived from 1840 to 1880, with its exaltation of human passions and its insistence on a polarized characterization of villain and hero. Realism, with its detailed, objective narrative, served well to reflect the economic and social changes in Argentina from 1880 to 1900. This Realistic novel also treated the financial crisis of 1890 and especially the fever of speculation that gripped the capital. It explored as well the theme of the immigrant, in particular the Italian, who swarmed to Argentine shores from 1870 to 1910. But while Argentina in transformation afforded a natural opportunity for objective realism, most Realistic novels were without sharp psychological insights. The characters portrayed, although often superficially interesting as types in a specific social milieu, lacked depth and convincing motivation. Of foreign origin, too, was the Naturalistic novel, which intended to transform the fictional canvas into a clinical laboratory to test out the doctrine of determinism. A movement started and cultivated by the French novelist Emile Zola, naturalism is fundamentally an extension of realism,but dwells on the more sordid and base elements of life, coldly observing how man succumbs to the dual forces of heredity and social environment. As we shall observe in Chapter 6, long after the cult of Zola had died out Gálvez belatedly introduced many Naturalistic elements into two of his social novels, *Nacha Regules* and *Historia de arrabal* (*Slum Story*).

Gálvez came of age around 1903, when the Modernist movement was renovating Hispanic poetry through its musicality, harmony of form, and deification of absolute beauty. Modernism was essentially a poetic movement, but manifested itself also in the novel and the essay. In part reacting against the excessive banality and sordidness of Realistic and Naturalistic literature, the Modernists sought refuge in fanciful and remote worlds of their own creation. By reason of temperament and innate artistic talent, Gálvez could not accept the basic tenets of Modernism. But one of his compatriots, Enrique Larreta, did fall under its spell and wrote the best and most representative Modernist novel of Latin America, *La gloria de don Ramiro* (*The Glory of Don Ramiro*), 1908. And although other authors, among them Manuel Díaz Rodríguez and Angel de Estrada, also composed Modernist novels, the movement in prose never took a firm hold. What persisted in the Argentine novel throughout the last decades of the nineteenth century and the beginning of the twentieth was the realistic, objective, earthy portrayal of the national scene. It is this tendency that Gálvez continued and with which he had greater success than any of his predecessors.[2]

Two Argentine novelists who spanned both centuries need to be mentioned to place Gálvez' work in proper perspective: Roberto Payró and Carlos María Ocantos.[3] Payró (1867-1928) brushed aside all sentimentality and idealism as he wrote of things Argentine. In *El casamiento de Laucha* (*The Marriage of Laucha*), 1906, Payró recounts the misadventures of a rascally youth who contrives a sham marriage to the owner of a rural store. With ironic realism recalling the Spanish picaresque novel, Payró weaves an ingenious plot enlivened by deft handling of popular speech. But Payró is on more common thematic ground with Gálvez in two volumes of short stories, *Pago Chico,* 1908, and *Violines y toneles* (*Fiddles and Barrels*), 1908, and a novel *Divertidas aventuras de Juan Moreira* (*Amusing Adventures of Juan Moreira*), 1910. These works derived from the same interest in national problems and social reform that inspired many of Gálvez' early thesis novels. Payró's stories are critical portraits of social and political life in Bahía Blanca, while his novel satirically portrays a malicious and devious professional politician. That Gálvez was directly influenced by Payró is not even suggested. Yet he knew Payró personally and read his fiction, and one of his works, the drama *Sobre las ruinas* (*Over the Ruins*), was published in *Ideas*. Payró was a popular writer in his day, in fact the best Realist of the early years of the twentieth century, until Gálvez made his appearance in 1914. But because of the limited number of novels and stories he wrote and their restricted scope, Payró could not make a serious impact on Argentine fiction nor be considered a national or representative novelist.

Neither could Ocantos (1860-1949), but for different reasons. True, it was Ocantos who made the first attempt to draw a complete picture of the contemporary Argentine scene in a series of novels. The publication of the twenty works of *Novelas Argentinas* spanned forty-one years, from 1888-1929. The series was an ambitious effort to present the gamut of Argentine life, from the cosmopolitan capital to the rural regions, from the hustle of crowded commercial streets to the monotony of the pampa, from the poor city dweller to the humble peasant. The variety of themes and personages is extraordinary; few segments of Argentine society escape Ocantos' pen. Yet for all his efforts, he never "struck home," never stamped his novels with the seal of the genuine Argentine spirit, difficult as that concept is to define. Perhaps his protracted absence from Argentina partly explains the aesthetic disassociation that the reader feels on taking up one of his novels. Then too, Ocantos' style and language are so completely in the mold of peninsular Spanish, so far removed from the Argentine vernacular, that the reader finds it difficult to establish any identity with the characters or the situations in the novel. In short, Ocantos portrayed Argentina as an outsider would, fully and dramatically, but lacking in authenticity and naturalness. Where Ocantos failed, Gálvez succeeded; that is, he made the Argentine scene convincing and believable in fiction. If Gálvez was not the first novelist to offer a well rounded picture of his country, he was without doubt the first to present it with a genuine and clearly recognizable Argentine flavor.

While Gálvez cannot be termed a "popular" writer, his works have sold better than those of any other Argentine novelist with the exception of Gustavo Martínez Zuviría (1883-1962), who wrote under the pseudonym of Hugo Wast. Yet Wast's purely literary merits as a novelist are so limited that no comparison with Gálvez is implied.

Although a fecund, popular, and entertaining writer, Wast's lack of aesthetic sensitivity has kept him merely on the fringe of the Argentine novel, preventing him from forming an integral part of its artistic development. The careers of Gálvez and Wast coincided chronologically, but their concept and execution of the novel were so divergent that they represented different worlds of fiction. Seeking only to indulge the reader's most basic emotions, Wast made no pretense of being a social reformer, psychologist, moralist, or even interpreter of his country's pattern of life. On the other hand, Gálvez fitted into all these categories, with varying degrees of effectiveness.

II *The Novel and the American Scene*

Other contemporary novelists, more talented and important than Ocantos and Wast, were adding new dimensions to Argentine fiction. Ricardo Güiraldes and Benito Lynch, with their novels of gaucho life, represented the dominant trend of *criollismo.* From Mexico to Argentina, from Chile to Puerto Rico, the *novela criolla,* or novel of the land, flourished from about 1920 to 1940 as an original and distinctive type of American fiction. What is more, Latin-American fiction blossomed for the first time with the *novela criolla,* which severed the ties that had bound it to European models and reflected the unique features of the American scene. Each country mirrored in its fiction the most distinguishable characteristics of its civilization, but not necessarily the most essential or representative: the jungles of Colombia, the *llanos* of Venezuela, the isolated mountain regions of Mexico, the pampa of Argentina, the tablelands of Bolivia. The novelist's awareness of America was thus transmitted to the reader essentially through its geography; that is, nature and the particular environment shaped by that nature were seen as primordial forces in the lives of men. Nature, all-powerful, hostile, and relentless, controlled hapless man and made him her victim, while man himself, with his conflicts and anguish, played a secondary role or was considered principally in terms of his surrounding environment. The Chilean critic Fernando Alegría correctly observes that the masters of the *novela criolla,* Ricardo Güiraldes, José E. Rivera, Mariano Azuela, and Rómulo Gallegos, "on humanizing the pampa, the jungle, the mountains and the rivers, actually dehumanized man." [4]

Clearly, Gálvez was aware of the *novela criolla,* but only by a forced extension of the term do his novels of city and provincial life come within the scope of its usual definition. He sees and portrays man in a social milieu rather than in an environment dominated by natural forces, although the same desire to awaken in the reader a consciousness of American reality is present in such works as *La maestra normal* and *La sombra del convento*. Then too, while the typical *criollista* novelist makes nature the real protagonist, Gálvez can never so completely submerge his characters in their environment that they fail to be the center of interest. He has too deep a concern for man and his psychological, spiritual, and religious qualities.

III   *Gálvez' Position in Fiction*

Many of Gálvez' works of traditional realism coincide chronologically with the flourishing of the *novela criolla*. Both types of fiction are vitally significant in the story of Argentine fiction. Yet Gálvez' position cannot be viewed principally with reference to the novel of the land; indeed, it does not rest on any preconceived notion of the nature of the Argentine novel or the direction it has taken. His position is best understood if we consider the period 1914-1938, when Gálvez wrote his most significant works, as a vast fertile field that was sown with a variety of productive seeds. And while the seeds disseminated by Gálvez might have touched and mingled with the others, they grew and flourished almost independently.

The novel of the land of the 1920's and 1930's overstayed its welcome. Obviously, there is more to Latin America than the confrontation between man and nature; implicit in man's existence is the struggle within himself, with his own psyche. In the period 1920 to 1940, the Latin-American novel was not ready to treat in depth man's inner conflicts. It first had to pass through the indispensable phase of identifying the reality that is America and feeling the uniqueness of that reality. And it did this well through the novel of the land. The convulsive shock of World War II, the increasing lack of effective communication and understanding among people, society's chaotic and illogical nature, have all contributed to exacerbate man's anguish and despair. Fortunately, the Latin-American novel has kept up with the times and in recent years has reflected this condition of mid-twentieth-century man, introducing themes of universal significance and probing the recesses of man's mind and emotions. The novel of the land has thus ceded to the novel of man.

This existential anguish found its most artistic voice in the novels of the Argentine Eduardo Mallea (b. 1903), whose persistent theme is the incommunicability and loneliness of man, his emotional mutism, his incapacity to give of himself. For his profound analysis of the human mind, Mallea is a significant literary figure, but the highly intellectual quality of his fiction appeals only to a select public responsive to the introspective novel, to the novel of inner conflict rather than of external action. The careers of Gálvez and Mallea partially overlap, but the two novelists have few artistic or narrative qualities in common. Mallea began writing fiction around 1935, when Gálvez was at the chronological midpoint of his career, but after he had written almost all of his best novels. Thus, when Mallea appeared, Gálvez' position was already firmly established and in no way weakened by the important thematic values and innovative narrative techniques of his younger compatriot. Even though Gálvez knew that the tide was changing, he held fast to his traditional view of the novel and felt no need to alter his technique, quite complacent over the success of his earlier works. Had Gálvez put down his pen in 1945 or 1950, when fresh breezes were blowing, he might have avoided seeing his subsequent works judged by new standards and new tastes in literature. But Gálvez wrote out of need, almost compulsively, as if fulfilling an inner drive. He continued writing long after his creative powers had diminished, long after he was able to contribute to the forward motion of Argentine fiction or even produce novels equal in artistry and significance to those of the earlier period. Although he died just nine years ago, his particular style of fiction passed away long before.[5]

CHAPTER 3

The Novelist's Craft

G ALVEZ conceived his fiction in the most straightforward and direct way possible. His novelistic art rests essentially on the desire to tell a socially significant story and create a social environment in the simplest and most intelligible terms. Singularly devoid of chronological inversions, narrative involutions, and all manner of stylistic artifice, his fiction invites easy reading and ready comprehension. His narrative technique is a simple and direct one, yet it is not ingenuous or superficial; it is perhaps too patent and predictable, yet in his best novels it rarely fails to engage our interest.

I *Technique and Style*

Gálvez was cognizant of these qualities of his fiction and not only took pride in them, but thought that innovative complexities of narration and style were not conducive to good novel writing. He considered the technical and verbal extravagances of writers like William Faulkner as inappropriate devices for fiction. In his volume of essays *El novelista y las novelas* (*The Novelist and Novels*), he adds:

> A writer's technique is a good one when it leads to the best possible understanding of the events and characters and to a facility in reading the book, so that the reader does not have to turn back at every step to know the identity of a particular character and what his relationship is to the others in the story.[1]

For Gálvez, lack of narrative clarity has no justification, either artistic or thematic. A novelist must not reproduce the chaos of life and the turmoil of man's mind by presenting an equally chaotic and clouded narrative. For this reason, he rejected Faulkner's *Absalom, Absalom,* charging that it would be unintelligible were it not for an annotated list of characters at the end of the novel.[2] For the same reason he thought that the cinematographic technique of John Dos Passos in *Manhattan Transfer* was entirely incompatible with the true nature of the novel.[3] We may conjecture that Gálvez would have considered Julio Cortázar's *Rayuela (Hopscotch)*, 1964, a futile exercise in narrative acrobatics if he had lived to read his compatriot's complex work.

Directness of narrative technique is clearly carried over into Gálvez' style. If this term implies the mode of writing and communicating peculiar to an author, then the dominant traits in Gálvez' style are naturalness, syntactical simplicity, and unaffected patterns of expression. His prose is free of rhetorical effects, of forced and artificial devices, of verbal excesses of any sort. Little concerned about the cold beauty and aesthetic values of many carefully wrought prose styles, he went to the other extreme to create a language stripped of literary pretense.[4] Yet his language is not elementary or tediously sophomoric; it is simple and unadorned without being prosaic. And what is equally important, the simplicity and naturalness of his style are not a studied manner adopted for artistic reasons; that is, simplicity is never a device in itself to strike our attention. Gálvez admits his dislike of a flowery or baroque style: "To clothe a novel entirely in artistic prose is erroneous. Each novel should have a distinct tone and movement, which can easily be lost when that novel is disguised in its new garments."[5] Most critics would agree that Gálvez applied these statements to his own style, although not all would commend it as much as Díez-Echarri when he affirms that "it is the ideal type for narrative prose, spontaneous, fluid, and without literary show."[6] The stark simplicity of the opening paragraphs of *Miércoles Santo* is illustrative of Gálvez' style:

The ringing of the bell drilled through the shadows that gathered more and more thickly in the dark house. Father Eudosio Solanas heard a second peal, and he could feel the urgent light which the sound had released in the hall shining on his eyes. He switched on his own electric reading lamp. The shadows that prowled around him darted back to the corners.

He heard the opening of the street door; footsteps; and, on the glass panel of his bedroom door, the three exclamation marks of rapping knuckles. His servant—who was also his sacristan—came into the room, clad in pyjamas with broad blue stripes. Solanas sat up in bed.

The rippling voice of the Galician servant announced a summons to confess a dying man in the Belgrano district. The priest did not wait to hear the name of the sick man. Rich and poor—all were equal in his eyes. He told his domestic to get out, and dressed as rapidly as the heat, his tiredness, and his vast bulk would let him.

It was only a little after eleven o'clock. He had gone to bed at ten. The next morning, Holy Wednesday, a grinding day was going to begin for him: hundreds of confessions, the prelude to the great Communion on Thursday. The high temperature would make his long hours in the oven of his confessional even worse. He would have to get up at dawn, and he had not slept at all yet. Sleep was just shyly approaching him—and here came a call for him.

He did not complain. A human being needed spiritual succour, and he was glad to help him to die well. His whole life was organized to the service of God and men.[7]

It is clear that the essence of Gálvez' simplicity is clarity and precision. It is not an aesthetic simplicity such as we find in Juan Ramón Jiménez' prose poem *Platero y yo* (*Platero and I*). For Gálvez, language in its most fundamental and obvious function should convey emotions and ideas, describe situations and social environments in an artistic but not unnatural fashion. Language has to provide exact and vivid verbal pictures; rarely should it strive to impress the reader with stylistic adornment. While such a position needs no justification, Gálvez felt he had to defend his style against possible attacks by those contemporary writers who relied heavily on linguistic devices. He states that the novelist who finds himself "surrounded by his fictional characters and stimulated by the intense desire to create and work does not stop to write in perfect prose or to fashion beautiful phrases, except in opportune moments." [8] Almost as an afterthought, and in less than convincing tones, he adds that the limited number of beautiful phrases he infuses into his own work surges forth from his pen spontaneously.

These aesthetic limitations in no way imply a lack of expressiveness or verbal force. With vigor and unobtrusive beauty, Gálvez can set a scene, portray an environment, describe the physical attributes of a character, or convey a psychological state. The reader may take pleasure in the lucidity of descriptive detail and the harmonious blending of these details into a unified narrative whole. There is no doubt that Gálvez is at his best when describing the elements that comprise the particular milieu of a novel. His observation is acute, his eye for detail keen, his sense of descriptive selectivity well developed. And he reflects these qualities in his language to produce a sharply focused picture. In his best writing, he possesses what in Spanish may be called *un estilo plástico*, a plastic style, one which is capable of making the reader feel, see, hear, and touch the essence of the scene depicted. His style is precise, exact, and what is most important, always concrete. Of the many passages that may serve to show this type of environmental description, a representative paragraph from *Nacha Regules* captures the incessant activity on the streets of Buenos Aires even at one o'clock in the morning, when the protagonist Monsalvat comes out of a cabaret:

At the first street corner he paused. People were leaving theatres and cafés, whirling away into the dark in taxis and automobiles. The trams were crowded. The crossstreets, of unpretentious apartment houses and second-rate shops, all darkened and asleep, were poorly lighted; but at its southern end, the center of the capital's night life dusted the sky with a golden sheen. Monsalvat turned in that direction, walking on mechanically till he came out on the brilliantly illuminated avenue. Through the immense plate glass windows of the cafés he could see the multitudes of little tables, and topping them, hundreds of human torsos gesticulating under thick waves of cigarette smoke, pierced with colored lights; while through the opening and closing doors, tango music broke in irregular surges, now strong, now weak. The street corners were sprinkled with men stragglers or survivors from larger groups of joy-seekers. Automobile horns, conversations in every tongue, the bells of blocked street cars, rent the lurid glow with resounding, impatient clangor. But in spite of all the animation and illumination of the theatre district, the merry-making had not the enthusiasm of the earlier hours. Only that irreducible minimum of vitality remained, that residue of joy-thirst, which survives evenings of revelry, clinging tenaciously to the later hours, and scattering over the after-midnight streets a pervading sense of weariness.[9]

II   *Models and Influences*

To speak of direct literary influences on Gálvez' work is to enter into difficult territory. We can never ascertain the extent of his indebtedness to a particular writer, nor even identify those writers who influenced him the most. More so than many of his contemporaries, he had a clear awareness of the relationship between his own fiction and the main currents of Latin-American and world literature. He wrote more out of literary vocation than out of literary genius. He carefully studied the craft of fiction and applied the lessons he learned to his own novels. Literary models served him less as mentors or guidelines than as artistic bedfellows with whom he liked to be linked in a common bond of fiction. Naturally, Gálvez' models possessed narrative and stylistic traits that were similar to those he intended to develop in his own fiction. Among the authors he admired, he felt closest in artistic temperament to Flaubert, Zola, Dostoevski, and Tolstoi. Despite their different aesthetic approaches to the novel, Gálvez saw in them many similar characteristics: narrative objectivity, striking realism, and directness of technique. What also appealed to him was their unpretentious artistic qualities, the absence of rhetorical and linguistic gloss. The traditional novel of the past century, with its faithful photographic depiction of reality and its precise, orderly construction, served as Gálvez' ideal. Not only was he firmly committed to the essential values of the nineteenth-century novel, but he felt that this type of narrative could not be surpassed as the most effective vehicle for presenting social and psychological conflicts.

For his depiction of sordid life in the slums of Buenos Aires, Gálvez admits the influence of a minor Argentine novelist named Francisco Sicardi, author of a five-volume naturalistic novel, *Libro extraño* (*Strange Book*), 1894-1902. Although Sicardi's influence is a very superficial one, Gálvez points out that he might not have written *Nacha Regules* and *Historia de arrabal* if he had not read *Libro extraño*.[10]

It is clear that Gálvez' artistic formation owes more to nineteenth-century French novelists than to any other single group.[11] He states repeatedly that Flaubert was his master, from whom he learned the technical art of composing novels. A direct offspring of Flaubert's *L'Education sentimentale,* Gálvez exuberantly writes, is Carlos Riga, the protagonist of *El mal metafísico.*[12] But if Gálvez quickly admits his debt to Flaubert for the clean, uncluttered narrative structure of his novels and the neat and methodical portrayal of character, he just as readily denies that his depiction of the national scene is any less genuinely expressed. His fiction remains distinctly Argentine despite the derivative nature of his basic technique and external composition. Gálvez was no servile imitator and perhaps he does himself a disservice by his insistent mention of Flaubert. Rather than conveniently spreading out a specific blueprint to follow, Flaubert, Maupassant, and Zola led Gálvez, as he himself suggests, to submit his literature to prescribed norms of art that restrained any narrative or stylistic excesses he might have employed.[13]

III *Imagery*

Gálvez' direct approach to verbal expression does not exclude the use of imagery, but it does limit it considerably. It is not that he deliberately shuns metaphors, similes, analogy, or other types of comparisons, but rather he does not feel the need to strengthen or embellish his words by frequently resorting to purely ornamental or even functional imagery. There is no thematic or linguistic pattern to his use of imagery and even a superficial classification is unnecessary. It is useful, however, to offer a few representative examples. Some of his images are rather commonplace and thus have lost their artistic value in transferring the reader's thought from one level to another:

Smiling, Linda was observing some couples . . . a Genoese round as a ball[14]

. . . her caressing voice . . . like clear velvet.[15]

Many images are more apt and pictorial, without being singularly imaginative:

. . . the slow words of doña Isabel, which, in the silence of the room, sounded like the monotonous flow of water.[16]

. . . small trees on both sides of the rails, very rigid like honor guards.[17]

Other images are more striking and add vigor to his prose, as in these descriptions of the Buenos Aires waterfront:

. . . the large, multicolored ships, the distant smoking chimneys, a black iron drawbridge, which, like a penknife being opened, was being raised after a train had passed over it . . .[18]

. . . the bare masts of the ships, which, when appearing from behind the dilapidated houses made of planks and zinc, looked like huge guns whose bayonets threatened the sky.[19]

Some of Gálvez' most effective images invest inanimate objects with human feelings, as in a description of a billiard table:

In this room there were two counters . . . and a melancholy billiard table that grew weary in frightful solitude . . .[20]

Nature, too, can provide an occasional fitting and beautiful image:

The moon covered everything with a thin fine dust of ashen whiteness.[21]

IV *Dialogue*

Dialogue is not a distinctive feature of Gálvez' fiction. As a means of revealing character and personality, it plays but a small role; the novelist relies almost exclusively on his own narrative. As a device to carry along the forward movement of the story, dialogue plays only slightly more important a role. In these two functions, the dialogue is seldom more than a recourse to vary the presentation of the story and to make the characters utter some words of their own. Except on rare occasions, such dialogue is neither inspired, ingenious, nor carefully thought out to serve as an effective novelistic technique. Yet dialogue in Gálvez' novels succeeds well in another function, as a forum in which characters voice their opinions on the social and political issues treated in the work. Dialogue thus becomes an added device to portray environment. Ideas clash, ideologies are expounded and refuted, prejudices are bared, diatribes are unleashed, social injustices uncovered and condemned. This type of dialogue is all the more effective because it is aptly integrated into the narrative material. It not only supports and enhances the narrative, but also provides an arena for testing the novelist's own feelings and beliefs in the heat of argument and counterargument. A notable virtue of Gálvez' technique is his ability to bring together under one narrative roof a varied array of personae and have them verbally interact one with the other. Some of the most engaging scenes in his novels are made more vivid by the dialogue that accompanies these confrontations. In *La sombra del convento,* the dialogue between José Alberto Flores and the younger Ignacio Belderrain or between Teresa Belderrain and her father dramatically points up the religious and cultural struggle between traditional ideas and liberalizing forces in colonial Córdoba. One of the most important scenes in *Nacha Regules* depends on an exchange of ideas between the idealistic reformer Monsalvat and a group of socially indifferent acquaintances. *La maestra normal* contains several poignant dialogues in which pertinent themes of the novel are discussed, defended, and attacked: provincialism, the spirit of colonialism, social and educational conservatism. The effectiveness of the portrayal of the Bohemian atmosphere in *El mal metafísico* rests in part on the free interplay of ideas and opinions among members of Riga's literary group and among the boarders at Señora Regules' pension.

On one occasion, at the home of his friend Eduardo Iturbide, Carlos Riga meets Dr. Isaac Lantero, one of the leaders of the Conservative Party and a professor in the School of Philosophy and Letters at the University of Buenos Aires. The conversation turns to the literary magazine *La Idea Moderna* that Riga and Iturbide have just helped to found. After looking at the Table of Contents of the first issue, Lantero disdainfully declares that he does not know any of the contributors. The dialogue continues:

"But, Doctor, they are all writers of prestige," said Eduardo.

And supported by Riga, who constantly intervened, he cited the merits of each one. Six had published books. . . . And the others were young men who were just beginning to emerge, writers for magazines and newspapers. . . .

"The truth is that I don't read unknown authors. There are no writers today."

And he added, in a slightly melancholy tone, his mouth full of names that he was citing: "Gone are the days of Sarmiento, Pedro Goyena, Avellaneda, Wilde, and others."

"If I may," said Riga. "Those people had literary ability, but they did not produce a single solid piece of work. Why do writers of talent waste their time on articles, letters of condolence, or toasts? What is important is the real work of literature, the book that lives and excites the reader."

"If you count only books," interrupted Eduardo, "not much will remain even of Sarmiento's works. The fifty-two volumes published by his relatives, abetted by the government, represent a national disgrace. Newspaper articles, letters, bad speeches. Sarmiento's only real book is *Facundo,* and even that work is very incohesive. It's an ordinary and badly written feuilleton, illuminated at times by flashes of brilliance."

Dr. Lantero was astonished. Eduardo's father smiled, and Lita listened attentively.

"Argentine literature is only beginning to exist," said Riga. "Previously, we had poets, almost all bad, and one or two historians. But where are they at present, the novels, the stories, the dramas, the plays, the books of criticism? Only now are they beginning to be written. Before, the professional writer did not exist; now he does. The men of those times, Doctor Lantero, were not artists, but idle politicians with no love of beauty or vocation as writers."

Lita listened to her friend with smiling gratification.

"And the fact is that here," added Eduardo, "politics is confused with literature." [22]

The language used in dialogues is generally that of the educated Argentine. With a few exceptions, Gálvez' central characters are cultured people who speak in an appropriately cultured manner, yet not without certain expressions that are singularly Argentine. While conscious of the Argentine vernacular, Gálvez does not make the peculiarities of speech intrude unnaturally in the dialogue. Although he does not deliberately seek linguistic effect through dialogue, he achieves authenticity by letting his characters speak in a natural and spontaneous way on subjects important to Argentines. That he also records such Argentine terms as *che, no hablás, seguí negando no más, macanudo, macana,* and *pucha,*[23] is too obvious a device for further comment. But even here, the use of such words is as carefully controlled as it is in good speech. When the common people or foreigners have speaking roles, the novelist at times tries to capture their peculiarities of language in brief bits of dialogue. The speech of El Chino, the pimp in *Historia de arrabal,* is punctuated with colloquial phrases and even transcribed phonetically when it differs from standard Spanish (78, 81). Similarly, the mispronunciations and barbarisms of the jockey in *La pampa y su pasión* (*Horse Racing Fever*), are noted with no small degree of amusement (96, 97). In *El mal metafísico,* the common errors of pronunciation made by Monsieur Durand, French patron of the arts, are indicated with special spellings of key words (130).

We should not belabor the subject of dialogue in Gálvez' novels; prolonged comment is not necessary. Yet a final word may be appropriate if only to reveal the novelist's obsessive concern for verisimilitude in his fiction. Writing about the real people that appear in his historical novels, such as the Argentine General Bartolomé Mitre in the Paraguayan War trilogy or the dictator Don Juan Manuel in the Rosas series, Gálvez states that "his true historical personages speak only words they actually uttered or wrote in letters or articles."[24] It is a bold comment obviously difficult to substantiate in some cases, but really unimportant in the final appraisal of these historical works.

V *Critical Comment Abroad*

The body of critical comment on Gálvez is voluminous. From 1914 until around 1938, few novelists in Latin America achieved as solid a reputation or enjoyed such wide popularity as Gálvez. Within Latin America, critics categorized him in several ways: the representative realist, the social reformer, the romantic idealist, the liberal novelist of the city. For many readers in foreign countries, he opened the door to Latin-American fiction. Spain came to know him well, first in 1913 as an essayist in *El solar de la raza,* and then a year later as a novelist in *La maestra normal,* which the distinguished Spanish writer Miguel de

Unamuno lauded in an article in *La Nación,* November 22, 1914. Spanish critics were as generous in their praise of his early works as were his compatriots. Affirming the essential unity of all fiction written in the Spanish language, Rafael Cansinos Assens stated with reference to Gálvez' historical novel *Los caminos de la muerte* (*The Roads of Death*): "A true master of the novel . . . who brilliantly holds his own with the very best of Europe and America. Among us, now that Galdós and Blasco Ibáñez are dead, his only rival is Concha Espina or Pedro Mata."[25]

Through translations Gálvez' name reached Europe,[26] and critics from France, Germany, Italy, and other countries were quick to include him in their small circle of Latin-American fiction writers. Treading on unfamiliar ground, foreign critics searched for answers, groped for styles, techniques, and themes which would help to define the Latin-American novel. In many cases, too much of their criticism centered around an ingenuous comparison with their own national fiction or that of other countries. To do otherwise would have been difficult; they were pleased to have discovered a worthy novelist writing in Spanish on this side of the Atlantic. One German critic,[27] for example, stated in 1923 that Argentine literature was not known and what really interested him was to find out what European influences had been significant on the younger writers in Latin America. Also in 1923, another German critic[28] commented that his countrymen were scarcely aware of the existence of an independent Latin-American literature, and the only authors known to them were the Nicaraguan Rubén Darío, the Argentine Manuel Ugarte, and the Brazilian Henrique Coelho Neto. For this reason, he was pleasantly surprised that a novel such as *Nacha Regules* came from the pen of an Argentine. For the president of the Budapest P.E.N. Club,[29] Sarmiento, Carlos Ibarguren, and Gálvez were the three greatest Argentine authors, and the outstanding talent among contemporary writers belonged to Gálvez, whose works, especially the trilogy on the Paraguayan War, should be known to Hungarians.

The novelist Stefan Zweig sent Gálvez a congratulatory letter after reading *Nacha Regules* in German. Zweig praised his "sharp realism, devoid of sentimentality yet full of feeling."[30] The German writer then added that he showed the novel to an editor of a Socialist paper, urging him to publish it serially so that readers would recognize the universality of social injustice and brutality. The German translation of *Nacha Regules* also moved the noted Danish critic Georg Brandes to send Gálvez a personal letter,[31] in which he indicated that the novel introduced him to Buenos Aires, although the seamy side of life that was portrayed seemed to him the same the world over. "I have had the same feelings toward humanity that are expressed in your novel," writes Brandes, "but I would not know how to express them with your eloquence." Brandes even saw the virtues of a Don Quixote in the protagonist's idealism and concern for the downtrodden.

In the United States, general interest in Gálvez' works has been no more than tepid outside a small circle of professors of literature. In all fairness, of course, we should remember that only in the last ten or fifteen years has enough Latin-American fiction been translated to English to awaken the reading public to its richness. Only two works of Gálvez' have been translated to English, *Nacha Regules* in 1922 and *Miércoles Santo* in 1934; such significant novels as *La maestra normal* and *Hombres en soledad* await an English version. When critical reviews of *Nacha Regules* appeared in the *Boston Transcript*, the *New York Times,* and the *New York Herald Journal,* they were quickly translated for Argentine readers in the daily *La Nación* of Buenos Aires. Among the small number of noted American writers who commented on Gálvez' fiction was Upton Sinclair,[32] himself the author of several novels of social protest. In Gálvez' stark portrayal of social exploitation and inequality, Sinclair recognized an affinity with his own works of fiction such as *The Jungle* (1906) and *The Metropolis* (1908).

Primarily, Gálvez interested foreign critics because of the intense realism of his novels and his ability to present a convincing and diversified picture of the Argentine scene without the thematic and psychological limitations of the regional novel. He attracted attention, too, because his novelistic technique was influenced by the French masters, with whom Europeans were often familiar. What critics traditionally expected in a novel—realistic detail, emotional experience, enjoyable reading, good story line, social and psychological insights—they readily encountered in his best fiction and responded favorably to it. One of his most enthusiastic French supporters even affirmed that through Gálvez "Argentine literature gained a place in world literature."[33] That French critics were generous in applauding his novels particularly gratified Gálvez, since in turn he admired modern French fiction and felt indebted to it for his own literary formation. Commenting on *Nacha Regules* when translated to French in 1931, one reviewer wrote[34] that Gálvez resembled Maupassant in his mode of narration and Tolstoi in his inspiration. Another critic,[35] writing in 1947, considered Gálvez the most important Latin-American prose writer, whose respected position with relation to the young generation of Argentine writers was similar to Theodore Dreiser's in American fiction. The device of comparing Gálvez to figures of universal fiction was used by many critics of other foreign countries. Although flattering to him, this type of evaluation is superficial or merely intuitive, lacking real analytical or textual support to make it critically valid. He was placed side by side with Zola, Flaubert, and Mauriac, with Tolstoi and Gorki, with Pérez Galdós and Blasco Ibáñez.[36] Gálvez' social themes, realistic technique, and moral and psychological probing recalled these masters and suggested, in bold overstatement, comparisons with them. How Gálvez applied his craft of fiction to specific novels will be the concern of subsequent chapters of this study.

CHAPTER 4

Conservative Provinces and Cosmopolitan Buenos Aires

IN his volume of essays, *El novelista y las novelas* (*The Novelist and Novels*), Gálvez comments that for some novelists the idea for a novel starts with the plot, for others with the characters, while for still others with "an atmosphere, a city, a farm, a house inhabited by many people" (p. 63). He adds that he belongs to this last group of novelists. Indeed, most of his best novels are those in which he focuses on a particular Argentine environment and peoples it with characters who for better or worse are caught in that milieu. Buenos Aires and the interior regions represented for Gálvez two opposing elements that he sought to portray objectively, with all their virtues and imperfections, advantages and shortcomings. Juxtaposed, these two environments form a huge canvas encompassing the basic features of Argentine life, particularly its struggle to shed the old and effete and don the new. Appropriately, as the scene of his first novel, La Rioja is symbolic of the source of Argentina's moral and spiritual strength, although its traditional, conservative values clash with the social forces of modern civilization. While lethargic and refractory to change, *La Rioja* contains the essence of "authentic" Argentina and should incorporate some of the progressive spirit of the capital into its pattern of life. This polarity of cultures within one nation is obviously not confined to Argentina; it is basically the stereotyped antagonism between the pure, idyllic, simple life of the country and the materialistic and perverted life of the city.

In portraying La Rioja in *La maestra normal* and Córdoba in *La sombra del convento,* Gálvez viewed provincial Argentina from the vantage point of the contemporary scene. What he saw was values and attitudes and institutions that had become outdated by 1920, but which had nurtured the life blood of Argentina from the days of the viceroys. The spirit of the provinces is incarnate in Raselda and the normal school principal in *La maestra normal;* it is in Ignacio Belderrain and in Father Mortero of *La sombra del convento*. In portraying Buenos Aires in *El mal metafísico, Nacha Regules,* and *Hombres en soledad,* Gálvez lamented the deterioration of those moral and spiritual values that had been the bulwark of Argentine life. For him the two worlds of Argentina—Buenos Aires and the provinces—might not have been so incompatible as they seemed; and indeed one of his constant personal struggles was to accommodate the two apparently antithetical environments into the spirit of *argentinidad,* or Argentinism.

Quite correctly, Fernando Alegría states: "There is no other Latin-American novelist of this period who attains such an essential union between man and his surroundings."[1] Physical environment is sharply and precisely defined, with just the right amount of descriptive detail. The milieu of La Rioja, Córdoba, or Buenos Aires is set squarely before the reader for him to feel and understand. Into such environments Gálvez places his characters, often with too strong a controlling hand, too firm a grip on their movements and ultimate fate. Yet it is not so much that he arbitrarily pulls the strings as it is that social environment greatly influences the characters and forces them into a circumscribed pattern of life. This same tendency leads one critic to state that Gálvez' characters do not undergo any appreciable change throughout a novel, but rather remain inalterable in their feelings and actions.[2] It is a valid observation, but this trait of Gálvez' fiction should be understood not as a narrative weakness, but as a method of character portrayal that relies heavily on environmental forces.

Around 1912, Gálvez first contemplated writing a series of novels revealing varied aspects of Argentine society.[3] The realization of that plan began in 1914 with the publication of *La maestra normal* and terminated in 1938 with *Hombres en soledad.* Gálvez' efforts were most intense in the first eight years, from 1914 until 1922, when he published *La maestra normal, El mal metafísico, La sombra del convento, Nacha Regules, La tragedia de un hombre fuerte,* and *Historia de arrabal.* These six works, together with *Hombres en soledad,* constitute the core of his ambitious project and made him Argentina's foremost writer of fiction. As a group, these seven novels are his best and most representative works. In the intervening years, between 1922 and 1938, Gálvez wrote mostly historical fiction and religious and moralistic novels, which broadened the base of his subject matter but did not stress the interplay of environment and character. The remaining pages of this chapter and the following one will be devoted to a study of the seven principal novels.

I   *Environment and the Normal School Teacher*

Otis Green[4] and Hugo Barbagelata[5] both point out that in the volume of essays *El diario de Gabriel Quiroga* (*The Diary of Gabriel Quiroga*), Gálvez had already conceived of Raselda as the protagonist of *La maestra normal* and considered La Rioja as an almost deterministic force in her life and in that of many other characters. Gálvez clearly states in *El diario:*

These cities, because of their characteristics and the poetry that lies within their soul, offer writers virgin worlds of raw material. Besides, I believe that nothing surpasses our northern regions as an environment for a novel. The realistic novel that narrates the intimate and silent dramas of obscure lives has a natural theme full of emotion and melancholy in the sad existence of each young woman of the provinces, those poor sentimental girls who live between languid dreams and wretched realities. (p. 147)

La maestra normal may be viewed from several angles, but all converge on Raselda's pitiful plight as a young teacher caught in the narrow, gossipy, and authoritarian world of La Rioja, still hostile to the influx of modern ideas. The story revolves around the seduction of an ingenuous provincial girl by a more sophisticated but selfish young man who has come to La Rioja to recuperate his health after a life of dissipation in the capital. The work is seen as well as a realistic, almost *costumbrista* portrayal of provincial life in La Rioja—the apathetic inhabitants, the pretentious petty officials, the Normal School and its rival the Colegio Nacional, the cafés, the holiday festivals. And in its deepest social significance, the novel may be considered an open attack on the weaknesses of normal school education, government bureaucracy, and parochialism.

When *La maestra normal* first appeared in October, 1914, it stirred no particular interest; readers received it cooly and critics' voices were still. Then, some months later, a laudatory article in a Buenos Aires daily by Miguel de Unamuno[6] launched the novel on the road to critical acclaim and popularity. What impressed Unamuno most was the novel's unflinching realism, particularly because it contrasted with the coldly aesthetic and intellectual qualities that characterized much of Spanish fiction at that time. Some Argentines, however, took exception to Unamuno's comments on the novel's strict adherence to reality. The most influential and vehement of these critics was the modernist poet Leopoldo Lugones, who a few days after Unamuno's article appeared wrote in the same newspaper that Gálvez was guilty of grossly distorting the environment of La Rioja.[7]

For Lugones, *normalismo* and provincial life were the targets of undeserved criticism. Never a friend of Gálvez', Lugones further insisted that the deliberate attack on the normal school teacher stemmed from the novelist's rejection of lay schools and his support of religious education. Yet despite these strictures, Lugones conceded that the novel was well written and revealed Gálvez' artistry and technical skill.

Lugones' comments, both the adverse and the encomiastic, created still further interest in *La maestra normal* and in Gálvez as an important, if controversial, literary figure. Resentful of the imputation that he was a foe of *normalismo*, Gálvez answered his critics. Defensively, he stated that Raselda was not a typical normal school teacher and therefore all criticism of the novel as a rebuke of that system had no validity. In her ignorance and professional incompetence, her romantic, dreamy nature, and above all her inadaptability to the environment of La Rioja, Raselda was a very unusual case. To the charge that *La maestra normal* gave moral offense to the reader, Gálvez rejoined that Raselda was the innocent victim of a deceitful and cowardly Solís, to whom she surrendered believing he would marry her. Then too, an imprudent servant and a coarse friend contributed to her fall. In truth, Gálvez is not even suggestive. He never alludes to physical contact, let alone the sexual act; at the close of Chapter VIII, the reader is simply led to understand that Raselda and Solís have become lovers. Besides, although Raselda suffers an abortion, the word itself is not used in the novel and reference to her condition is always made with the utmost discretion. What is more important, Gálvez wanted his work to be considered a Catholic novel since "the feeling of sin and remorse is evident and because Raselda's story contains a moral and Christian lesson." [8] Lacking religious faith, Gálvez added, the protagonist was less able to resist sin.

Bitter controversy from other quarters accompanied the unprecedented success of *La maestra normal.* Conservative elements both in Buenos Aires and the provinces attacked Gálvez for his seemingly unsympathetic treatment of provincial life. A group of normal school teachers was so enraged that it asked for his resignation as Inspector of Secondary and Normal Schools. A few provincial cities, led by La Rioja, organized official meetings to discuss the objectionable features of the book. Even in Paraná, Gálvez' birthplace, there was a public demonstration against the novelist. Provincial and urban newspapers eagerly covered the polemic. To combat the novel, a group of writers in Catamarca founded a magazine ironically called *La Maestra Normal*. Indeed, the center stage in Argentine fiction in 1914 and 1915 was all Gálvez', but the vehemence of some of his attackers was to pique him for many years to come.

*   *   *

Far more significant than the simple plot of *La maestra normal* is the wealth of environmental detail and character depiction. The milieu is graphically drawn from the moment that Julio Solís steps off the train at La Rioja until the epilogue informing us that Raselda continues to lead the same monotonous and wretched life she led before meeting Solís. Gálvez captures well the lethargy and drabness of life in La Rioja in descriptive passages such as the following:

The city seemed to have a sweet sadness, in spite of the color that the orange trees and the roof tiles put on the grey background of the mountain. Only a few people were walking in the streets. In some doorways, the servants, dressed in their Sunday best, were looking at the passersby with strange curiosity. From time to time a vehicle went by, slowly, almost unwillingly, bounding on the miserable stone pavement. Their echoes were lost in the solitude of the streets. The passengers were men; occasionally one saw a vehicle with women inside, all seated up front. And both men and women were serious, silent. Here and there, a dark woman with penetrating eyes leaned indifferently at a balcony window. When Solís passed, the women looked at him in surprise and followed his steps. Houses stood side by side with ruinous adobe walls, the remains of the old city destroyed by earthquakes. The drainage ditches, as if monotonously reciting a prayer, produced an indefinable tediousness. (p. 22)

Three local settings in La Rioja, all part of Solís' life during his stay in that city, enable Gálvez to display his gift for descriptive narrative: the pension, the pharmacy shop, and the *confitería,* or café. Doña Críspula Paredes' pension, where Solís lives upon his arrival in La Rioja, provides a fitting introduction to the city and some of its inhabitants. Gálvez carefully describes the owner, her daughter Rosario, the servant Candelaria, and several guests, among them a businessman named Galiani and a young pianist Pérez, director of the Conservatory. For each character the novelist pens a few revealing lines, which at times border almost on caricature. Doña Críspula is depicted in these words:

. . . a broad and pleasant woman, rather short, with a large stomach and a moon face. Her cheeks shone brightly like billiard balls. On her chin she had a mole, with long and curly hairs on it. She spoke with the steadiness and the slowness of a badly turned-off faucet and nodded to the rhythm of her words. Her double chin shook like gelatine. She must have been around fifty and she laughed heartily for any reason, especially at the end of a paragraph. (p. 9)

The description of Galiani picks up apparently minor but significant details to reveal character:

He had a very thick and somewhat drooping moustache, hair combed in waves toward the front, and sharp, mischievously smiling eyes that looked askance. When speaking he would twist his body affectedly. He tried to be sleek and amiable. He wore several rings and, in an upper vest pocket, a large gold watch with a very thick chain, at the end of which was an assortment of medals and amulets to ward off evil. (p. 17)

Gálvez' initial observations about Pérez center on his marked speech defect:

Nice fellow, cheerful disposition, always ready with stories and jokes. But, how he stuttered! Of course, sometimes it was funny; but other times he was to be pitied and everyone was embarrassed for him. (p. 17)

Gálvez interrupts his description of the pension just long enough to tell us of Solís' background: his illegitimate birth in Paraná; a lonely and neglected childhood, similar to Raselda's; a life of vice in Buenos Aires, with some intermittent periods of serious study and writing; and finally his tubercular condition that brought him to the more salutary climate of La Rioja. At Don Numeraldo's pharmacy, Solís meets the principal of the Normal School, Ambrosio Albarenque. The description of the locale and the people who regularly congregate there in the social and intellectual atmosphere of a typical *tertulia* is vivid, natural, and wholly integrated into the action of the novel. These evening *tertulias* afford Solís his only chance to discuss ideas and literature, an activity that formed so vital a part of his life in Buenos Aires. Gálvez is particularly adept at depicting this type of intellectual atmosphere, in which he brings together a group of people with conflicting ideologies and aesthetic tastes to interact with each other. Despite the novelist's claim to complete objectivity, his own viewpoints frequently emerge, sometimes through characters who act as his spokesmen, like Gabriel Quiroga, other times through the verbal tone and content of the

narrative, as in his criticism of Albarenque. Referring to this latter
character, Gálvez says ironically: "Like all perfect pedagogues, the
principal was anticlerical and a positivist" (p. 26). The founder of
positivism, the Frenchman Auguste Comte, is Albarenque's god:

It was rumored that when the principal arrived in La Rioja he
privately used the Comtian calendar: month of Homer, month of
Shakespeare. The jokes of some insolent people forced him to abandon
it. Comte's catechism and Torres' pedagogy were the only basic things
in human knowledge. (p. 27)

One of Albarenque's political and academic foes is Don Numeraldo
himself, at one time superintendent of public works, portrayed as
pseudo-intellectual, mundane, and aggressively sociable. There are brief
descriptions of other members of the *tertulia,* although most of them
play no active role in the development of plot. They serve exclusively as
colorful characters in the setting. Among the most regular participants
is Nilamón Arroyo, prominent physician who also teaches classes in
natural science at the Normal School. A beloved and dedicated teacher
with a disarming sense of humor, he is one of the few professors who
has effectively resisted the high-handed practices of the principal. Don
Nilamón is Gálvez' ideal of the traditional family doctor, compas-
sionate, self-sacrificing, and above all responsive to his patients' needs
regardless of their ability to pay. The gregarious small-town politician
wrapped up in local affairs is sketched in the figure of Sofanor Molina.
Affable and popular, he is the best teller of risqué stories in La Rioja.
Partly because of his position as city manager, he is also one of the
most worldly and best-informed citizens and ably serves his community
as carrier of the latest news.

Absent-minded, hen-pecked Eulalio Sánchez Masculino, once a
successful lawyer, now earns most of his living from real estate, but also
holds the chair of ethics and citizenship at the Normal School. Don
Eulalio spends only the last few days of each month at the pharmacy,
much preferring the gaiety and fun of the hotel *confitería,* fully
equipped with a bar and billiard table. If the *tertulia* caters to the
intellectual élite, the *confitería* serves the populace seeking no more
than companionship to while away a leisure hour or two. Although by
temperament and culture Solís is more attracted to the *tertulia,* he
finds satisfaction in spending some time at this popular *confitería.*
Gálvez frowns at the idleness of the *confitería,* which he sees as part of
the pervasive inertia of provincial life. Yet, for all its defects, it is the

"soul of the city . . . a breeding place for budding revolutionary activities, a combination of agora and forum" (p. 46). Like all newcomers to the closed society of La Rioja, Solís at first is the object of curious interest, perhaps even suspicion. Besides, inasmuch as he is a *porteño*, that is, from the sophisticated capital city, he incurs the envy of those whose dreams of visiting or living in Buenos Aires can never be realized. Among the many people Solís meets at the *confitería*, perhaps the most interesting is Miguel Aranjo, an eloquent orator and staff writer for the liberal newspaper in town. Ill-tempered and impatient, on one occasion he engaged Sofanor Molina in a duel; on another he even challenged Albarenque, but the contest was never carried out.

Besides the pension, the pharmacy, the *confitería*, and the Normal School itself, many other places are similarly sketched to provide a comprehensive picture of provincial life. Few parts of La Riojan society, from the wealthy home of Gamaliel Frutos to the humblest shack at the edge of the city, escape Gálvez' attention. The physical environment, the moral atmosphere, the types of inhabitants, and the overall social climate are all drawn with sharp narrative strokes. In its completeness, the depiction of La Rioja is unequalled in any of Gálvez' novels. One of the most colorful descriptions is that of the feast of the *Niño Alcalde* (p. 222), celebrated each year by the indigenous population of the outlying districts of La Rioja. In describing the merriment, the music and dancing, and the general orgiastic atmosphere pervading the festivities, Gálvez shows us a much neglected regional culture lying beyond the main roads of Argentine civilization.

If Raselda, despite her sin or perhaps because of it, gains our compassion, Solís strikes us as a morally dishonest, almost contemptible character. While we sympathize with Raselda's romantic longing for happiness and personal acceptance, we fail to respond to Solís' search for a more meaningful life away from the crassness of Buenos Aires. Certain circumstances in Raselda's life draw her to us from the very beginning: an unhappy childhood as a result of her illegitimate birth; an unfortunate love affair shortly before she meets Solís; a mediocre intellect that is unable to cope with the demands of her profession; and above all, a docile, insecure nature that makes her an easy victim of the authoritarianism of Albarenque, the malicious gossip of the townspeople, and the selfish motives of Solís. Her inefficiency as a teacher within the inflexible normal school system arouses our sympathy rather than our criticism. Paradoxically, Raselda's weakness becomes her most engaging quality. Solís, too, is weak, but his weakness is reprehensible, for he is an egotistic and irresponsible man who holds his acts

accountable to no one but himself. Several critics[9] have mentioned the
novel's felicitous blending of realism and idealism; that is, the faithful
depiction of La Rioja on the one hand, and Raselda's romanticized
vision of life within the confines of her drab surroundings, on the other.
In a sense, too, Raselda's idealism receives its crushing blow when the
opportunistic Solís refuses to marry her and leaves La Rioja. Abandoned and in disgrace, Raselda is a pitiable figure at the close of the
novel. As for Solís, alcoholic and still gravely ill with tuberculosis, he
fails to achieve fulfillment or happiness on his return to Buenos Aires,
although he secures a routine position as a writer for an afternoon
newspaper.

Many cogent scenes alternating dialogue and narrative contribute to
the sense of movement and vital energy of the novel. One scene
(pp. 85-87), for example, points up Raselda's inadequacy as a teacher
and the lack of humanity on the part of her supervisor, Señorita
Rodríguez. The scene is one of the best in the novel, poignant, full of
pathos, vigorous yet effectively controlled. One morning, apparently
without previous notice, Señorita Rodríguez enters Raselda's first grade
class. Upon seeing her, the young teacher is overcome with fright and
becomes silent, unable to proceed with her teaching. Annoyed with
Raselda's weakness, the supervisor orders her to continue the lesson.
Gálvez notes:

Raselda's face flushed, she bit her lips, looked at her superior,
lowered her gaze. Irritated, Señorita Rodríguez nervously tapped her
foot on the floor. "I've come to observe your class," she stated, with
authoritarian brusqueness and folding her arms as if getting ready to
wait.

Uneasy, Raselda manages to continue the geography lesson but gives a
poor performance in a subject generally her best. To Raselda's timid
and lifeless voice the pupils respond in kind; they are bored, they
slouch in their seats, they fidget with their pens. Then, with a
condescending smile, the supervisor sardonically adds: "But, señorita, I
don't see why you are so frightened. I'm not the bogey man." And if
this is not enough, she proceeds to humiliate Raselda by taking over
the geography class herself. The lesson is superb, her methodology
flawless, her discipline excellent; but at the same time her action
debases Raselda before her own pupils and destroys the little
confidence she has in her worth as a teacher. Her mission completed,
the supervisor turns haughtily to Raselda and says: "This is the way you

should conduct your class. I have given a model lesson only to encourage you, since I do not have to teach." After Señorita Rodríguez leaves, Raselda reflects on her own deficiencies and accepts them, but fails to understand the harsh behavior of her superior. And no sooner does Raselda resume the day's activities than the pupils revert to their apathetic and undisciplined behavior.

The merits of *La maestra normal* go beyond the depiction of environment, the portrayal of a wide variety of characters, and the harmonious union of these two elements. They lie even deeper than the sympathetic study of Raselda and her relationship to Solís. What is most important to the novel's success is the fine equilibrium between pairs of novelistic elements: Gálvez' objective narration and the not infrequent intrusion of his own point of view; descriptive portrayal of character and character revelation through environmental association, dialogue, and plot development; collective presentation of the external milieu and the individual conflicts of persons living within that milieu. The novel reads well and never becomes tedious, principally because of a constant shift of narrative focus and the cumulative presentation of Raselda's involvement in the provincialism of La Rioja and in the pettiness of her professional surroundings.

II *A Writer's Struggle in the Big City*

From the provincial life of *La maestra normal,* Gálvez proceeded to the cosmopolitan atmosphere of Buenos Aires for his second novel, *El mal metafísico (The Metaphysical Ill),* 1916. In his first two novels, then, he treats two opposing forces in Argentine society—the static, repressive provinces and the dynamic capital. Yet rather than present a composite picture of Buènos Aires in one single novel, Gálvez preferred to limit his principal focus to the literary world and treat only peripherally other aspects of the capital. As the story of Gálvez' generation, *El mal metafísico* contains much autobiographical material of the period 1900-1910. The novel concerns a young writer's inadaptability to the crass materialism of Buenos Aires, the daily struggle of a romantic dreamer against the cruel indifference of a big city. Like *La maestra normal,* it juxtaposes the most earthy realism and the most exalted idealism. In its broadest sense, the work concerns the debasement of cultural and aesthetic values in the face of utilitarian concepts of life imposed on modern society.

While the success of Gálvez' first novel was not immediate, *El mal metafísico* struck a responsive chord from the moment it appeared and within two months all copies were sold out. It has continued to be one of Gálvez' most popular works and has been translated into many foreign languages. If *La maestra normal* provoked the wrath of provincial and conservative factions in Argentina, *El mal metafísico* was readily accepted by all because its theme and content could offend no one. Yet it is not a bland novel, written without conviction or social commitment. It subscribes to an ideological position, but the object of its protest, the mass of culturally insensitive *porteños,* is so indeterminate that it does not stir up heated controversy. Besides, who can object to the youthful aspirations of a struggling poet or to efforts to have a more enlightened public?

The protagonist, Carlos Riga, is obviously Gálvez himself as a young and promising writer at odds with his social and cultural surroundings. But whereas Gálvez was able to overcome his adverse milieu and gain success, Riga can offer little struggle and eventually succumbs.[10] He lacks the will to achieve, the emotional disposition necessary to overcome his environment; he suffers from what Gálvez calls the *mal metafísico,* that is, the illness of "dreaming, creating, producing beauty, meditating" (p. 226). In Julio Solís of *La maestra normal* can be found some of the same *mal metafísico,* although because of his selfish nature he arouses no sympathy. During his early years spent in Buenos Aires, Solís tried to veer from a life of dissipation, but he was weak-willed and unable to resist. Riga's weakness goes deeper than Solís' and affects his every act. He is the prototype of the person Latin Americans like to call an *abúlico,* a term referring essentially to lack of will power but which also connotes social inadaptability, moral intransigence, incommunicability, and even inertia.

The environment depicted in *El mal metafísico* is almost exclusively that of the literati of Buenos Aires. The cast of characters is very numerous and varied.[11] The wealth of detail concerning their personal lives, the description of their meeting places, their conversations and discussions, their hopes and frustrations, all provide an interesting and significant background for the novel. Gálvez does not hide the fact that *El mal metafísico* is a *roman à clef,* with many of the principal literary figures of the day clearly identifiable.[12] The most significant of these are Abraham Orloff, in reality the short story writer Alberto Gerchunoff, and Eduardo Iturbide, in real life Ricardo Olivera, who co-founded *Ideas* with Gálvez. Less important figures among Riga's acquaintances are Alberto Reina, in reality the novelist Atilio Chiappori, Dr. Escribanos, in life the controversial essayist José Ingenieros, and Moisés Roca, a thin disguise for the critic David Peña.

With the exception of Iturbide, these characters play only a passive fictional role, entering only marginally into the main story line. In this respect, they are quite similar to the array of secondary characters found in Solís' pension, the *confitería,* and the *tertulia* in *La maestra normal.* Since Gálvez depends heavily on environmental detail, the poet's literary companions are essential to the novel, yet their lives impinge only slightly on Rigas'. He talks with a host of characters about literature and art, about politics and life, sustains long polemics with them, even shares his thoughts and feelings, but then goes his own way alone to face up to personal conflicts and seek answers to his most urgent problems.

The shattering of Riga's idealism and his moral ruination through successive stages of disillusion and frustration constitute the thematic unity of the novel. Several scenes portraying this breakdown are particularly moving and worthy of note. One of Riga's closest friends is Eduardo Iturbide, skeptic and pseudo-intellectual, scion of a well-to-do family of Buenos Aires. Eduardo's sister, Lita, meets Riga and the two fall in love, but the sharp difference in social status and the poet's economic instability cause her parents to oppose the courtship. To thwart the budding romance, Lita is simply sent off to Europe, despite her objections. Riga is crushed and now realizes that his idealism affects even his affairs of heart. In a well-structured and poignant scene, Riga bids Lita farewell on the deck of the steamship that will take her to France. Inhibited in the expression of her feeling for Riga, all she can utter is "Study and write; send me your poems from time to time. You will continue to write, won't you?" (p. 112). Amid the gaiety, pretension, and sophistication of Lita's family and friends, Riga feels inferior and unimportant and her words seem directed to a small boy who is not to be taken seriously. To add to his anguish, as he mills around the crowd he overhears two women mocking Lita's involvement with a penniless poet. Riga becomes indignant, not so much because the women have berated him, but because he senses that his world of poetry and culture and idealism is toppling:

He remained motionless for a moment. Life, youth, love, he had lost everything because God made him an artist. Why wasn't he a bourgeois, a run-of-the mill lawyer? Then Lita would have been his. (p.115)

Gálvez is especially effective in the next few pages of the novel as he narrates how Riga deadens his grief in drink. He enters a bar on 25 de Mayo Street after a brief walk from the pier along the Paseo de Julio.

As if to point up his state of depression, the description of Riga at the bar is punctuated four times with his words of supplication: "Waiter, a whiskey." When he finally reaches home, he is comforted by his companion Ardonio, who views his conduct as more than a mere drunken spree, but a symptom of his inability to cope with reverses, of his propensity toward the *mal metafísico*.

Riga is torn between his need to forget Lita to preserve his emotional health and his need to remember her as a source of comfort. With lyric expressiveness Gálvez writes the concluding paragraph of Part I:

His face, like a tragic sky, was tortured by repressed tears, and his anguished features had flashing nervous movements. He remained standing for a few seconds, silently, motionless, leaning on his friend. But finally he could bear it no longer and threw himself headlong on the bed. And there the storm that was seething in his soul was unleashed in a shower of tears, sad and sobbing tears, long tears, tears that forever washed away in its depth the beauty of a young life. (p.118)

On one occasion Riga's idealism, coupled with uncompromising professional integrity, costs him his job. At the time, he is a writer for a militant political newspaper, earning a small salary but satisfied that he is practicing his profession. Since political writing holds no real interest for Riga, he balks at an assignment to do a series of articles on controversial issues. Although he manages to write the essays, none is suitable for publication. A few of his short stories and poems do appear, but the publisher questions Riga's usefulness to the paper. To put the poet to the test, he orders him to write a denunciatory article attacking the president of Argentina, with particular reference to a certain San Luis affair. Riga's knowledge of the matter is negligible and even after consulting several accounts of it feels incompetent to draft the article. Besides, his conscience prevents him from launching such a harsh verbal attack. Recognizing his predicament, Riga speaks to a fellow worker named Fernando, a stubborn pragmatist who denies the place of honesty or integrity in journalism. While Fernando affirms that the journalist should not have any ideas of his own and should write only what suits his newspaper best, Riga can write well only through firm conviction. Reluctantly, the poet puts together an uninspired article on the San Luis affair, so deliberately vague and aesthetically refined that it fails to fulfill the revengeful purposes of the publisher. Without waiting to be fired, Riga promptly resigns. The scene ends on a note of ironic criticism as Orloff, also on the staff of the paper, admits to Riga that he has already penned twenty articles on the same subject without sorting out the facts, weighing opinions, or comprehending its real meaning.

Riga's utopian romanticism leads to his destruction. His idealism is irreconcilable with the cult of materialism in Buenos Aires and clashes with the vice and corruption of a large metropolis. Riga is witness to this depravity as he himself struggles with poverty and disease and walks the streets in despair; later, he too sinks to the lowest level of degradation and becomes a hopeless alcoholic. The reader also perceives this ugly slice of *porteño* life in the person of Nacha Regules, whose mother owns the pension where Riga once stayed. Fatherless since early childhood, trapped in a discordant home, Nacha took a lover as her only refuge from adversity. After giving birth to a stillborn baby, she tried to get a respectable job, but low wages forced her to work as a barmaid in a cheap cabaret. Gálvez paints her sympathetically as a victim of her environment, of a callous and unjust society. Riga beseeches Nacha to befriend him and minister to him, to unite their wretched lives. Out of compassion, Nacha agrees; they live together for three years, she working at menial tasks, he occasionally writing an article. When Nacha loses her job and becomes destitute, she leaves Riga to fend for himself. Rather than suffer hunger, Nacha turns to prostitution, as readers will later find out in the novel that bears her name. Gálvez' message is clear, but idealistically naïve: two basically decent persons are morally destroyed because of society's indifference to their needs.

Without Nacha, Riga is lost. His only source of emotional comfort gone, despondent and infirm, he winds up in a sanatorium. After showing some improvement, he is released, but one day he spies Lita and her fiancé in an art exhibition and old but still cherished memories begin to haunt him. The romantic soul of Riga can never envisage her married to someone else. When, some time later, Lita learns that Riga is on his deathbed, she is overwhelmed with emotion. If circumstances were different she could have felt a deep love for the poet, certainly a far greater love than she feels now for her future husband. And her fiancé's feeling for her, as Gálvez puts it, is "trivial and only skin deep" (p. 223), not the true, poetic, almost mystical love professed by Riga. This same type of spiritual love will appear in several of Gálvez' subsequent novels—Monsalvat's love for Nacha in *Nacha Regules,* Mauricio Sandoval's platonic relationship with Susana de Olózoga in *El cántico espiritual,* even Victor Urgel's liaison with Elsa Brandán in *La tragedia de un hombre fuerte.* It is clear that for Gálvez spiritual love is part of the larger, more encompassing spiritual life which all Argentines should strive to cultivate.

Appropriately, *El mal metafísico* bears the subtitle "A Romantic Life," for Riga's frequent display of exalted emotion smacks of traditional romantic sentimentality. On one occasion, at Lita's extravagant birthday celebration, Riga explains with juvenile candor that he cannot bring her a gift because he is poor. Instead, he dedicates some verses to her as a declaration of love:

In elegant Alexandrines, he spoke of Lita as of the fairy princess, and at the end stated in a tragic tone that to lose her would mean the shattering of his illusions, the disaster of his existence,death. (p. 82)

This romanticizing of Riga's feelings may seem incompatible with the realistic framework of the novel, but it serves to insulate the poet from his baneful environment and thus heighten the contrast between his inherent idealistic nature and the cold commercialism of Buenos Aires. What Gálvez does in this and other novels is to temper the crudeness of environmental realism with an idealized portrayal of selected characters within that environment. Raselda of *La maestra normal* and Monsalvat in *Nacha Regules* are two other characters treated in this fashion. Owing to the strength of the novel's theme, the idealization of Riga's character does not detract from his credibility as a fictional creation, but rather enhances our empathy for him. Artistically, the important thing is that through Gálvez' depiction of Riga—however sentimentally overdrawn it may be—the reader gains rich insight into the literary world of the 1900's and the people who shaped it.

El mal metafísico is a veritable forum for literary and cultural points of view. The presentation of these ideas, which fills many of the most rewarding pages of the novel, is achieved as much through dialogue as through narrative exposition. Although at times lengthy, this dialogue is well integrated into the main story of Riga's idealistic struggle and follows naturally from the concerns and interests of the characters. Iturbide, the most carefully delineated of Riga's companions, provides stable leadership for the young bohemians. His cynicism and aristocratic nonchalance about traditionally accepted values of art and culture provoke some members of the group and stimulate others, but always place him on center stage. With Iturbide's support, Riga founds the journal *La Idea Moderna,* which carries the pretentious subtitle "Revista de Filosofía, Literatura, Historia, Arte, y Crítica." More than anything else, the poet wants the magazine to reflect his generation's ideas about the "spiritual rebirth" of Argentina. It is clear that *La Idea Moderna* is in reality the journal *Ideas*, which we recall Gálvez and Ricardo Olivari founded in 1903. In fact, the two journals follow parallel histories. Riga soon realizes that Iturbide's (like Olivari's) initial enthusiasm has waned and that he himself has to put together the entire magazine. Like Gálvez, Riga finds that many contributors are unreliable or tardy. And both journals suffer a premature demise after showing unusual promise.

When not meeting in cafés or salons, the literary group convenes at Iturbide's apartment, where he lives with his mistress Margot, a charming French woman with broad cultural interests. Iturbide's insistence on the superiority of French culture and the mediocrity of Argentine makes him a forerunner of Gervasio Claraval, one of the central figures in *Hombres en soledad*. A frequent visitor to Iturbide's home is José Alberto Flores, born in colonial Córdoba, but a resident of the capital for some ten years. A misdirected and neurasthenic youth, he is to return to Córdoba as the protagonist of Gálvez' next novel, *La sombra del convento*. Just as frequent a visitor is the provocative Gabriel Quiroga, whom the reader already met in *La maestra normal* in a very minor role.[13] As a defender of those traditional provincial values that need to be retained to form the modern Argentina, Quiroga meets the strong opposition of Iturbide, for whom the provinces represent cultural barrenness and stagnation. A heated discussion begins when Quiroga announces his forthcoming trip to the provinces "to know my country, to become saturated with Argentinism and with tradition, to de-Europeanize myself a bit, to rid myself of the foreign coat of whitewash I have on" (p. 143). Mockingly, Iturbide responds:

"Bah! For that buy yourself a poncho and some riding boots on the Paseo de Julio and go to the National Theater. Besides, if they remove the foreign whitewash from us, we shall smell like Indians." (p. 143)

Riga, who spent the first fifteen years of his life in the provincial city of Santiago, remarks that he will never entertain the thought of returning to his birthplace, where all one does is while away the time at the *confitería*, play cards, and take afternoon naps. When Quiroga counters ironically by asking Riga what he does in his "attractive" and enlightened Buenos Aires, the poet is left without words and realizes the futility of trying to explain his own position. Then, as narrator, Gálvez interposes his own remarks, casting his vote quite obviously with Quiroga in his defense of provincial spirituality.

As Jefferson **Rea Spell** points out,[14] Riga's life is all the more pathetic because he is the only one of his literary group who refuses to compromise with reality. Although many of his companions are likewise idealists and dreamers, they do not hestitate to cast off the burden of their ideology to suit social and economic exigencies. Riga is alone in the intensity of his suffering and alone in his defeat.[15]

III   *Tradition and Old Córdoba*

For his third novel, Gálvez returned to the provinces, to the "learned" city of Córdoba, the seat of Jesuit influence and Catholic dogmatism. The intent of the work is patent: to attack religious authoritarianism and narrow-mindedness that choke intellectual vitality and impede progress. By no means incompatible with Gálvez' deeply religious feeling, his rebuke of the Church's intolerance and austerity is essentially a censure of outmoded colonial attitudes that persist in modern society. The conflict presented, as Otis Green states, is a temporal one; that is, "the reconciliation of the old—the colonial—Argentina with the new, or at least of the acceptance of the new, and an effort to retain some vestige of the virtues of the old." [16] As the prototype of an archconservative, religiously dominated city, Córdoba is unmatched. At the beginning of the twentieth century, three important elements in that city defined its character: the National University, which still had not opened its doors to modern scientific thought; the Jesuits, who had founded the University in 1613 and sought to maintain their control by thwarting the influx of new ideas; and the small minority of intellectual and social reactionaries who supported the Jesuits and the University in order to retain their privileged position. Gálvez knew the city well, understood its essential nature as well as he did the bohemian circles of the capital. In fact, if stripped of its repressive colonial atmosphere, Córdoba might have held just as much attraction for him as Buenos Aires. In his memoirs, he comments that "if I should leave Buenos Aires to live elsewhere, I would go to Córdoba." [17] His acquaintance with the city dates from the period 1907 to 1910, when he made frequent trips to the northern provinces as Inspector of Secondary and Normal Schools. Besides, his future wife's delicate health obliged her to spend long periods of time in salubrious mountain regions, where Gálvez would frequently visit her. One winter he sojourned a month in Córdoba, residing in a hotel that faced the Plaza San Martín.

What is portrayed so effectively in *La sombra del convento* is the city of Córdoba caught in the grip of the powerful conservative sectors of society, and in particular the personal struggle of José Alberto Flores against these forces.[18] As noted before, Flores appears in a fleeting role in *El mal metafísico,* having just returned to Buenos Aires from Europe, where he had lived for several years. As a young man Flores led a dissolute life in his native Córdoba, incurred large gambling debts, and at one point attempted suicide. To avoid a scandal, his father cautiously sent him off to Europe. *La sombra del convento* takes up Flores' life when he is back in Córdoba to seek inner composure and emotional fulfillment. Like Gálvez himself, Flores lost his faith, but continued to see in religion a source of aesthetic pleasure and happiness. His disavowal of Catholicism, his skepticism, and his liberal ideas on the role of science in education make him unacceptable to Teresa Belderrain's family as her suitor. There is no more fanatical defender of Catholic dogma than the elder Belderain, who sees in Flores nothing but evil and defilement. When Flores openly attacks established authority in Córdoba, especially the Jesuits, Belderrain's wrath knows no bounds. Intimidated and distraught by her father's intransigent attitude, Teresa finds no other solution but to enter a convent. Flores' latent religious feelings are rekindled as he realizes that the only way to gain favor with the Belderrains and persuade Teresa to abandon the convent is through spiritual regeneration.

His ultimate conversion, his marriage to Teresa, and the death of Belderrain provide some of the most emotionally intense moments of the novel. Critics are of two minds regarding Flores' redemption. The majority would agree with Díez-Echarri[19] that his conversion is logical and convincing, fully compatible with his nature and with the events of the novel. A few critics see a basic weakness in the ending, particularly the docility with which the outspokenly liberal youth surrenders to the Church.[20] Yet no one would deny that the stages of Flores' rebirth of faith are carefully and extensively portrayed and constitute a cohesive sequence of events. While his wish to marry Teresa is the overriding motivating force behind his conversion, the initial impetus comes from a feeling of personal guilt over his Aunt Isabel's illness. It is she who provides a home for him in Córdoba and for whom he has a special fondness. Thus, when she falls ill upon learning that her nephew dared to print an article against the Church, Flores feels the pangs of remorse and repents his reckless action. And at his aunt's supplication, he even reads her portions of the *Imitation of Christ,* which deeply moves him and calms his troubled spirit. More significantly, he recognizes the consoling value of religion on contemplating his aunt's placid resignation in the face of death. Moreover, a kindly, enlightened priest, Father Rincón, who ministers to Aunt Isabel at her home, tries to persuade Flores to reaffirm his Catholic faith, to accept Catholicism despite its dogma and its rigidity. In answer to Flores' question, "Do you think, Father, that I can be a Catholic? " Rincón answers solemnly: "Yes, I think so, and I even think you are already a Catholic. The only thing you need to do now is to kneel down" (p. 151). He further assures Flores that the Belderrain family will forgive his transgressions and Teresa will leave the convent once he has renewed his faith. A new life begins to open its doors for Flores; he exults in the joys of religious devotion and in the prospect of marriage to Teresa. The venerable Córdoba is no longer inimicable to him. Its cathedrals become havens of inspiration and hope, its devout inhabitants objects of his love and understanding. The religious processions, the symbols, the clerics, and all the other outward signs of religious fervor draw him closer to the awesome traditions of Córdoba. Aunt Isabel's sudden turn for the better shortly after Flores confesses his sins is more a symbolic occurrence than a significant point in the plot. Yet for Flores, there is no doubt that his spiritual rebirth has contributed in no small measure to his aunt's recovery.

For all his renewed faith, Flores still rejects the dogmatic and the ritualistic in Catholicism. The novel's message is that he succeeds in making an appropriate reconciliation between spirituality and the ties and exigencies of formal religion. He represents the birth of a new, liberal Catholicism, in consonance with the needs and demands of a modern society. His struggle for social and religious change reflects the whole process of cultural revision that Gálvez would like to see in Córdoba. And the death of Ignacio Belderrain obviously connotes the passing of outdated Córdoba—not the passing of its traditional cultural values, but of those pernicious religious and cultural elements in its society that Flores attacks throughout the novel.

Next to Flores, the figure of Belderrain is the most carefully drawn and interestingly presented. As the ideological antagonist of Flores, he is despotic and unyielding; as Teresa's father, he is willful and overbearing. The forceful presentation of these qualities in narrative and dialogue makes Belderrain an engaging character despite the unsympathetic treatment Gálvez accords him. In one of the novelist's typical character delineations, informative, matter-of-fact, and devoid of verbal adornment, the reader is first introduced to Belderrain. A professor of civil law at the University and a judge of the Supreme Court, he is one of the most respected men in Córdoba. His harsh religious intolerance he equates with total spiritual devotion; his irascibility he equates with righteous indignation at those who would controvert Catholicism. Civil marriage is anathema to him, a form of "repugnant concubinage" (p. 28), and when he served as provincial delegate to the National Congress, he strongly opposed giving it legal sanction. Buenos Aires is such a den of iniquity and irreverence for him that he banishes all its newspapers from his home. His domestic tyranny extends to all members of the family, but it is Teresa who is most adversely affected. Belderrain's youngest son, Francisco Javier, faintly portrayed in the novel, is the only child who has ever rebelled against his unwarranted severity; when on one occasion he fails to appear on time at the dinner table, his father wrathfully orders his place setting removed and never put back again. The one happy figure in the Belderrain household is the oldest daughter Asunción, whose liveliness, humor, and humanity sometimes even break through the somberness of the Córdoban atmosphere. Whereas Asunción is a vital and dynamic figure even though she plays an insignificant part in the novel, Teresa fails to register any impression on the reader, although her role as Flores' fiancée is an important one. As a fictional creation, Teresa is lifeless and insipid, passing through the novel in some of the poorest scenes in a major work of Gálvez', her real character never emerging from the conflict that pulls her in two directions.

In the portrayal of Teresa's older brother Ignacio, the novelist shows consummate skill. Cut from the same pattern as his father, he personifies the perpetuation of religious intolerance in the younger generation of intellectuals. It is true that the sharp dichotomy between liberal and traditional forces in Córdoba is well defined in the figures of Flores and Belderrain, representing two different generations. But Gálvez recognizes, too, that the differences may be further brought out by juxtaposing the ideologies of two young men of the same generation. While Flores contends with both the elder and the younger Belderrain, it is the son with whom he can more closely identify and with whom he carries on the more personal battle. Ignacio becomes Teresa's protector and an even more vitriolic enemy of Flores than his father. On one occasion, Ignacio delivers a speech at the University attacking modern science, which for him is not even worthy of consideration as a branch of human knowledge, since it consists solely of falsehoods and unfounded theories that no institution of learning should sanction. Flores is appalled by the ideas contained in Ignacio's address, finding it incomprehensible that such a narrow, medieval viewpoint can be given currency in twentieth-century Córdoba: "There is nothing more imprudent, antiquated, and barbaric than to try to shut a university off from modern currents of thought" (p. 65).

A direct confrontation between the two youths brings their antithetical worlds into clearer focus. Ignacio censures José Alberto on two counts: for fomenting discord in the Belderrain family by courting Teresa, and for tenaciously defending his position against traditional Catholicism. Irately, José Alberto shouts out that the real cause of Teresa's unhappiness is the fanaticism of her father and brother. He underscores this statement with the words: "Yes, ridiculous and criminal fanaticism. And this you call the Christian spirit. The Christian spirit is the law of love and you practice the law of hatred" (p. 117). Violence ends the scene, the most dramatic in the novel, as José Alberto, enraged over Ignacio's repeated insults, strikes him with a leather riding strap.

Through Flores' eyes, as he lives the terrible moments of personal conflict, the reader comes to know each corner of Córdoba. Shortly before returning to his faith, he leisurely walks through the outlying districts of the city in search of emotional repose:

He left the lake and continued walking. He reached the end of the cliffs next to the park. Below, in the hollow, lay the city. The high, grey cliffs descended in deep folds, without a plant or stone. They resembled ancient ruins, remains of gigantic walls. Stretching below, the city took on a bluish tone. José Alberto observed how the multitude of towers and domes that revealed the Catholic soul of Córdoba stood out in the bright daylight, which spread over the houses like whitish smoke. He knew his Córdoba well and could distinguish each church. From his vantage point, the towers and domes of the churches near Plaza San Martín seemed crowded together. A short distance from the Cathedral of Córdoba he spotted the colonial church of the Theresian Order; nearby, the black towers of the Jesuits loomed high. Behind the Córdoban cathedral, Santa Catalina appeared to be no more than a pale blot, and on the two huge domes of Santo Domingo . . . remained the last radiance of glazed tiles. Just to the south of the plaza, scarcely visible, San Francisco seemed to hide its humble face; and to the north the tall thin towers of the Merced looked like two columns; and close by the intricate mass of the Church of Pilar. (p.159)

Once, at the suggestion of Aunt Isabel, José Alberto goes to the Cathedral of San Francisco to hear a sermon:

It was given outside, in the temple's small plaza. A huge crowd filled the plaza and the adjacent streets. Most of the people were men and women of the lower classes. In order to get a space, some women had come early, carrying food which they would later reheat in a small pan. A foul smell of grime pervaded the air. The lights from the lamps near the church were extinguished. Only the large candles that surrounded a calvary lit up the scene. Large groups of men and boys had climbed up the iron fences around the square. In the darkness, the details of the church facade were blurred. José Alberto managed to jostle his way a few yards through the crowd. The three crosses rose up in the corner formed by the two solid masses of the convent building. (pp.160-61)

In novelistic technique, *La sombra del convento* is among Gálvez' best works, perhaps second only to *La maestra normal.* Its total effect is one of structural cohesion and narrative unity. The thematic exposition is clear and direct and leaves no doubt as to the religious and social issues involved. The evocation of Córdoba is remarkable in its descriptive force and its relevancy to the theme of the work. The reader senses Córdoba and feels his own emotional involvement in the conflicts presented. The depiction of the ascetic colonial atmosphere is almost as complete as that of La Rioja, with arresting descriptions of the surrounding mountains, churches, squares, houses, colorful streets and parks, and the somberly attired inhabitants. All of this descriptive material is carefully blended into the narrative so that environment and plot grow together harmoniously and complement each other. A few secondary characters are portrayed solely to enhance the verisimilitude of the environment and provide the novel with a sort of *costumbrista* realism. Such is the case with the old bell ringer, who is as much a part of Córdoba as the church itself or the Belderrain family. More interesting, even though slightly exaggerated, is the characterization of Doctor Suárez, with whom Flores converses during the ceremony of conferring university degrees. A strong traditionalist, Doctor Suárez is professor of ecclesiastical public law. With Flores lending an attentive ear, he reminisces and describes the classic ceremony in which the bishop handed diplomas to the graduates and repeated *gradus doctoratus in sacrae theologiae facultate per impositionem hujus pilei* (p. 52). Ostentatiously, he showers his speech with these and other Latin phrases, which furnish an added image of solemnity and traditionalism to the scene.

CHAPTER 5

Further Directions in Realism

I The Generous Prostitute

IN 1917, Gálvez published his most popular and commercially successful[1] work, *Nacha Regules*, the story of a prostitute. The social reformer that Gálvez fancied himself to be is nowhere more patently seen than in this work.[2] It is a thesis novel and its propagandist qualities tend to weaken its literary merit, although not quite so appreciably as J. R. Spell suggests.[3] There seems little doubt that Gálvez had been nurturing his ideas on society's ills long before he set out to write *Nacha Regules*. His youthful support of socialism, Tolstoian Christianity, and even an attenuated form of anarchism attested to his serious concern for the ultimate purposes and goals of government and society. Then, too, his dissertation on white slavery for his law degree revealed still more concretely his sympathy for the downtrodden and the underprivileged. Yet he was far from being a man of action, certainly not a militant crusader for reform. His position on social justice in *Nacha Regules* is more ideological than practicable, to the extent that Fernando Alegría faults the novel on the grounds that Nacha's redeemer, Fernando Monsalvat, is more a literary than a human figure.[4] Yet few would label Nacha and Monsalvat as artificial, unconvincing creations. At worst, Gálvez may be guilty of that romantic idealization of character that we have already noticed in Raselda, Carlos Riga, and José Alberto Flores. Clearly, Nacha, the generous, victimized harlot, and Monsalvat, the apostle of good deeds, are fictional exaggerations of types encountered in real life. Although extreme cases, they are capable of moving us emotionally because they form part of a believable environment which is seen at the same time as their unrelenting antagonist. Redemption through love is the obvious theme of *Nacha Regules*. More particularly, the novel is the story of Nacha's moral regeneration through the efforts of Monsalvat, whose unselfish love for the unfortunate prostitute is matched only by her own deep feeling for him. The plot hinges on his persistent attempts to free Nacha from the grip of prostitution and concubinage and have her accept him as savior and spouse. His frustrations over the realization of these plans and Nacha's elusiveness give the novel its vitality and movement.[5] The lives of Nacha and Monsalvat must be understood as two disparate courses struggling to meet and blend. The polarity of these two lives that depend on each other for emotional fulfillment provides the initial interest in the novel as well as its thematic thrust.

We recall that Nacha appeared first in *El mal metafísico* as Riga's lover, later to abandon him when she could no longer endure their poverty. Some time before her affair with Riga, Nacha was seduced by a boarder at her mother's pension. Fear of scandal and her mother's wrath compelled her to leave home and live with her seducer, who abandoned her just when she was about to bear his child. Even her mother rejected Nacha and refused to take her back. After the death of her infant child, she again tried to live a decent life and did obtain honest employment as a sales clerk, but the low salary, poor working conditions, and the bad influence of co-workers forced her into prostitution. With a sense of her own destiny, Nacha relates to Monsalvat:

"There was no help for me. What could I do? I struggled from week to week; but debts, hunger, the need of clothes to put on my back, the luxury I saw around me! ... One day I told a girl who worked in the store and was a friend of mine that I would do whatever she advised ... and she took me to a house she knew." (p. 63)

Repelled by the indecencies of her profession, Nacha gave up prostitution after six months and eked out a living at various odd jobs. While working as a waitress in a dance hall, she met Riga. When the liaison ended, Nacha returned to the streets and became the kept woman of the lecherous El Pampa Arnedo. It is at this point in her life that *Nacha Regules* begins, specifically when Monsalvat, in a cabaret, defends Nacha from mistreatment at the hands of Arnedo and his gang. Although moved principally by compassion, Monsalvat is also physically attracted to Nacha. Her emotions toward Monsalvat are at first ambivalent; she feels admiration and sympathy for him, yet is afraid and unsure of his true motives.

The real relationship between the fallen woman and her redeemer begins when Monsalvat surprises Nacha at her apartment, and, after winning her confidence, explains his mission to help her. For the first time she feels that someone has taken a personal interest in her tragic life. She pours out her soul to Monsalvat, picturing herself as a victim of society, of men's lust and cruelty, of family circumstances. Her own confused feelings are nowhere more poignantly brought out than in her refusal to heed Monsalvat's plea to change her way of life. When he asks her whether she is repentant, she responds negatively, rationalizing that there is no need to be since "I did not intend any wrong" (p. 64). Although Nacha wants to leave her calling, she cannot, for she is held down by the threat of poverty and the vicious hand of Arnedo. "It's Fate. I was destined to be a bad woman" (p. 64), utters Nacha as a final summation of her plight. But Monsalvat's earnest concern kindles in her a spark of rebellion against her present condition. And when he points out the physical and emotional ravages of sin, a frightened Nacha desperately cries out for his assistance. Yet this positive reaction is quickly cut short as the immediate reality of her life with Arnedo regains its sinister hold. To help Nacha, Monsalvat understands that he now has to be the stronger of the two antagonistic forces in her life.

In Monsalvat, we see the acme of Christian virtue and self-sacrifice. More importantly, he is a heroic figure of romantic idealism in a milieu of sordidness and misery. Every facet of Monsalvat's background and character is deliberately selected to heighten the effect of his apostolic mission. Although from an affluent family, he is sensitive of his illegitimate birth and feels it weakens his social position. Introverted, even withdrawn, he suffers from the same sort of spiritual loneliness that surrounds many characters in Gálvez' fiction. Although for a time he was employed in a law office and wrote an occasional newspaper article, of late he has reproached himself for his useless and egotistic life, devoid of humanitarian concerns. In a tense scene at the home of his friend Ruiz de Castro, Monsalvat shows that he is emotionally disassociated from the rich, pretentious guests at the gathering. The haughty disdain and snobbishness of two young women particularly anger him, while their reactionary social philosophy becomes intolerable to him. The intent of the scene is obvious: to present the world that is diametrically opposed to Nacha's and callously unsympathetic to it. What is more, for Gálvez it is the segment of society responsible for the plight of the lower classes yet reluctant to propose social reform for fear of relinquishing its privileged position. At one point, after one of the guests denounces all workers who use the strike as a weapon, Gálvez describes Monsalvat's feelings:

Monsalvat could listen no longer. He was quivering with indignation. Usually serene, quiet, and incapable of hating anybody, he would at this moment have enjoyed strangling the individual who was taunting him so flippantly. Now he realized that all the men and women around him were his enemies, representatives of his old outworn ideas, of prejudices which he had come to abhor. On their faces he could see only insolent satisfaction with good living, a proclamation of inhuman selfishness, a spirit of evil, hypocrisy, pride, an absence of all human sympathy. (p.79)

Monsalvat's concern for social justice and economic opportunity in part grew out of his own family background. His mother, a modest worker in a dress shop, was seduced by Claudio Monsalvat, became his mistress, and gave birth to two of his children. Complacent and arrogant, the elder Monsalvat did not hesitate at the same time to take a wife within his own social circle. Although he provided some property for his mistress during their relationship, he died intestate. Several years later, owing to legal complications and incompetent lawyers, she was left destitute and dependent on her natural son Fernando for economic support. Fernando's sister Eugenia was a victim of parental neglect, soon became involved with the same El Pampa Arnedo, and succumbed to prostitution. Eugenia never assumes an active role in the novel, but rather mirrors the circumstances of Nacha's life and her fate as a fallen woman. The similarity between Nacha and Eugenia exacerbates Monsalvat's anger and makes his mission of social reform even more meaningful to him. Yet the coincidence is too contrived to be convincing as fiction and the reader is unmoved by Eugenia's situation, despite the fact that Monsalvat combs every house of ill repute in the capital trying to find her.

By common consent, *Nacha Regules* is considered a Naturalistic novel, one that follows the cult of Emile Zola and shows how the relentless forces of heredity and environment bear down on hapless man and eventually crush him. But the work arrived belatedly on the scene. As a movement, both in Europe and in the Americas, Zolaesque naturalism lasted from 1870 to around 1905. By 1922, when *Nacha Regules* was published, it had passed from the literary scene as a formal mode of novel writing, although its influence is felt even today. Naturalism in Latin America never took a firm hold, but its basic tenets were followed by a few novelists, notably the Argentine Eugenio Cambaceres (1843-1888) and the Mexican Federico Gamboa (1864-1939). Gálvez definitely was familiar with Zola and his *Nana,* most likely did not read Gamboa, and undoubtedly did not read his own countryman Cambaceres. Our novelist not only denies having followed in the path of Naturalistic fiction, but in his usual role as upholder of the Catholic faith sees his work as essentially Christian in its "compassion, resignation, sacrifice, love of neighbor." [6] These qualities, implies Gálvez, run counter to the very nature of the objective and scientifically detached Naturalistic novel. Despite his protestations that he is no disciple of Zola, *Nacha Regules* exhibits so many of the essential characteristics of the Naturalistic novel that it is difficult not to place it under that rubric. One important reservation has to be made, and that is Gálvez' deep humanitarian feelings toward the wretched souls he depicts. He is not the insensitive, unemotional narrator who views humanity with disdain and callousness. Unlike most Naturalists, he extends a helping hand to the fallen and the unfortunate and infuses a ray of light into their lives. Gálvez' attenuated naturalism is akin to that of the Spanish writer Emilia Pardo Bazán (1840-1915), in that their strongly religious beliefs made them unwilling to reject free will entirely in favor of a deterministic philosophy. Placing *Nacha Regules* in the niche "Naturalistic novel" is merely a formality of criticism, important though it may be in identifying it in its broadest terms. Far more useful is the fact that those thematic and narrative elements associated with naturalism form the distinctive features of the novel and contribute most significantly to its meaning. These elements are treated in the following pages.

To observe more effectively the interaction of heredity and environment, the Naturalists had to tilt the scales, all too often presenting the lives of poverty-stricken men, sick and wretched people, degenerates, alcoholics, prostitutes, and pimps. They also had to set the scene in the dirty and vice-ridden city street, the crowded avenues of industry, the insalubrious factory and mine, the squalid home, and the house of ill repute. Buenos Aires as the huge, impersonal, industrialized home of teeming multitudes of humanity is the only city in Argentina which can convincingly serve as the setting for a Naturalistic novel. Nacha's world is the world of poverty, squalor, and corruption, of social inequality, of economic strife and exploited workers. The brutality of El Pampa Arnedo, the callousness of the madams and the procurers, the pathetic lives of the prostitutes in Florinda's establishment, as well as the sordidness of Nacha's existence, all contribute to the Naturalistic milieu of the novel. [7] Then too, Gálvez follows the Naturalists in the careful documentation and quasi-scientific recording of subject matter, presenting detailed case histories of two prostitutes besides Nacha and Eugenia. Determinism is not only an important element of naturalism, but an indispensable one as well, and Gálvez' characterization of Nacha subscribes to this doctrine as closely as possible within the framework of Catholic belief. But it is clear that Gálvez' determinism gives greater weight to environmental factors than to hereditary ones in forging the destiny of Nacha. Yet despite the pervasive determinism of the novel, Gálvez is more the idealistic social reformer than the exponent of scientific naturalism. In creating Nacha as a plaything of fate, he is more interested in exposing social ills than in evolving a deterministic portrayal of a prostitute.

While it is true that *Nacha Regules* is a novel of social protest, it does not even suggest a program of social reform. Like so much of Gálvez' ideology, the novel observes carefully, records passionately, criticizes vehemently, but fails to offer solutions to problems or even constructive comments. Yet the theme of social injustice is a vital undercurrent throughout the novel and involves three basic elements: society's guilt for prostitution, vindication of Nacha as a fallen woman, and Monsalvat's altruism both as Nacha's redeemer and a champion of the oppressed. As we have noted, the initial impulse for Monsalvat's humanitarianism came from his feeling of guilt at having accomplished nothing significant in a society that cried out for reform. He was awakened from his lethargy one day as he observed the police brutally disperse a crowd of workers protesting low wages and poor working conditions. But what angered Monsalvat the most was that the well-to-do, the middle class, and even the merchants remained silently indifferent to what was happening in the street. Months later, after his encounter with Nacha in the cabaret, Monsalvat meets his old friend Amílcar Torres, who vituperatively indicts society for creating the conditions which force young girls into prostitution. Torres' words cause Monsalvat to reflect on the abject lives led by Nacha, his sister, and his mother. Some time later, at Ruiz de Castro's party, Monsalvat echoes Torres' sentiments, but his indignation falls on deaf ears and provokes the wrath of many guests. For some, his liberal views on labor and government border on anarchism. Nettled by Ruiz, who serves as the novelist's ideological disputant, Monsalvat utters an earnest plea for the prostitute:

"No, not degenerates: victims! Many of them try to work. Pitiful salaries, with debts they can't avoid, drive them into the power of vice. A few of them may, indeed, be degenerates—offspring of feeble-minded or alcoholic parents for whom, in a more roundabout way, we are perhaps just as much to blame. But, on the whole, the cause of the social evil, as of other evils, is in me, in Ruiz, in the man going by there in that automobile, in the factory owner, the store proprietor, in the criminal laws which give a sanction to economic injustice, in our moral ideas, in our conceptions of life—in our civilization, in short. The fact is, we have no human sympathy, no sense of justice, no pity. Countless numbers of these poor girls might still be saved, because they have not yet completely lost their self-respect. But what have we ever done to rehabilitate one of them? Do we ever go into the places where they live with any purpose but a shameful one? Do we ever extend the hand of Christian fellowship to the outcast? Can any one of us say that he has never, even by tacit complicity, helped to bring about the degradation of any woman?" (pp. 117-18)

From words to deeds, or at least attempted deeds. Monsalvat wants to make major improvements in the tenement house he owns by mortgaging the property. His tenants will have to vacate their flats during reconstruction and then return to them after completion of the work. But his noble intentions meet with the resistance of most tenants, who misunderstand his generosity and interpret his plan as a devious way of raising the rent. What makes them refuse Monsalvat's proposal is more than ignorance; it is the awful burden of oppression and exploitation, of resignation in the face of misery. Years of ill treatment at the hands of landlords have insensitized their feelings and destroyed their will to fight back. Ironically, a prostitute is one of the few tenants who trust Monsalvat and believe in his project. The analogy between the lot of his tenants and that of Nacha is painfully obvious to Monsalvat: a compelling deterministic force drags them down to their present condition and prevents them from seeking to improve it.

Not a few of the many turns of plot involving the relationship between Monsalvat and Nacha are melodramatic and exaggerated. What is more, while *Nacha Regules* is one of Gálvez' most important social novels, it is weak in insights into human conduct. It focuses more on what the two protagonists stand for than on what they are as persons, apart from their social roles. Psychological analysis remains shallow, no more than a superficial explanation of actions, feelings, and beliefs. What is lacking is the deep probing of behavior and motivation, of cause and effect, to which the reader would be responsive since the personages are intrinsically interesting. Although Nacha is a sympathetic character to whom we cannot fail to react emotionally, we are unable to distinguish her own person, fraught with special problems and conflicts, from the anonymous mass of prostitutes Gálvez defends and would redeem. Nor does Monsalvat exhibit much more individual character than Nacha; we never really know him as a person who transcends the figure of the apostolic redeemer. It is not that we do not believe Nacha and Monsalvat as fictional characters, but rather that we are compelled to accept them exclusively in terms of the novel's social thesis.

In the pathetic irony of the Monsalvat-Nacha interdependence lies perhaps the novel's greatest aesthetic appeal. Motivated by compassion and love, Monsalvat asks Nacha to be his wife, thereby risking further alienation from the middle- and upper-class society with which he is still outwardly linked. Although she loves him, Nacha magnanimously rejects his proposal, for she cannot let him sacrifice himself. At the same time she wants to be worthy of his love and lead a good life. For most of the novel, Nacha is obviously the weaker and the more dependent one in the strange relationship, for she desperately needs the strong emotional support that only Monsalvat can give her through his generosity and love. But the final scenes of the novel reverse the situation. After economic setbacks, failure to implement his modest program of social reform, and lack of progress in effecting a change in Nacha's life, Monsalvat is shattered physically and emotionally. He is committed to a sanitorium, gains some peace of mind, but continues to suffer the agony of unfulfillment. He is convinced that no single crusader like himself or even group of crusaders can bring about social change, but that the concerted effort of people from all levels of society is the required formula for success. Monsalvat escapes from the sanitorium, but he is now a poor soul, penniless and infirm, wracked with a sense of hopelessness not unlike Nacha's state of mind as a lost woman. In spirit he has become as weak as Nacha, and in a scene of painful irony even asks an indigent acquaintance for sustenance. Ironically too, Monsalvat is forced to take up lodging in a run-down *conventillo*, or tenement house, the same type of dwelling he once owned and intended to improve. Destitute, one day he meets Nacha in a streetcar and her voice brightens his gloom. But Nacha restrains her natural tenderness toward Monsalvat because she is accompanied by the man she is about to marry, a rich rancher for whom she has little love. The tables are turned, for now it is Nacha who feels compassion for the distressed Monsalvat. This chance meeting influences her to break relations with her fiancé, even though by so doing she denies herself financial security. When she finally returns to Monsalvat, she becomes the strong partner who has to sustain him emotionally. After Monsalvat becomes blind, his dependence on Nacha is absolute. She asks him to marry her, knowing that he needs her even more than she does him. Thus it is Nacha who is now willing to sacrifice herself out of pity and affection for Monsalvat. At first he refuses to accept the sacrifice, but then realizes that in this act lies her final redemption, that only in suffering with him, blind and ill, can she fully regain her self-esteem. In agreeing to marry Nacha, Monsalvat thus achieves his greatest triumph, for he not only becomes her redeemer but the one to whom she will dedicate her newly-found life.

II *Depravity and Viciousness*

Encouraged by the success of *Nacha Regules,* Gálvez mixed the same ingredients of prostitution, concubinage, and environmental determinism in his next novel, *Historia de arrabal (Slum Story),* 1922.[8] But it falls far short of *Nacha Regules,* mainly because the portrayal of the two protagonists is much less developed within the novel's social context. Demonstrating the same type of attenuated naturalism that we have seen in *Nacha Regules, Historia de arrabal* relates how a vicious youth forces an innocent girl into prostitution and mercilessly controls her every act. It is clear that Rosalinda Corrales is of the same stripe as Nacha and El Chino is the counterpart of El Pampa Arnedo.[9] But whereas Nacha's subjugation by Arnedo is just one element of plot, although an important one, Rosalinda's complete surrender to El Chino will become the central issue of *Historia de arrabal.* It is a brief, compact, and tightly written work that is no more than a skeleton of a Naturalistic novel in the Zola fashion. The plot is thin, character delineation is terse and at times even impressionistic, narrative and descriptive detail sparse.[10] Yet the novel's link with naturalism is obvious in many of its brief descriptive touches. The ills of an industrialized society, frequently treated in naturalism, are symbolized in the *frigorífico* or meat-packing plant, whose products represent a principal source of revenue for Argentina. Gálvez observes:

The walls and roof of the plant, whose massive buildings stretched out along the river like an immense, towering, and compact white mass, had taken on in that May dusk suave blue-like hues. Through the short entrance passage of paving stones, flanked on both sides by huge whitewashed walls, the workers were leaving for the day. (p. 7)

For Gálvez, these men are the oppressed masses that society exploits, and as the novelist follows them home he notes the wretched conditions of the *arrabal,* the slum neighborhood. This is where El Chino and Rosalinda live. The exploitation of the workers breeds the city slum, which feeds on a feeling of hopelessness and indifference on the part of its tenants. In the best descriptive pages of the novel, Gálvez first gives a general view of the *arrabal* and then the specific apartment inhabited by El Chino and Rosalinda. Although Gálvez seeks narrative objectivity, his own emotional involvement and even compassion break through in a way that is not characteristic of the nineteenth-century Naturalists. In the following paragraph describing the *arrabal,* note the abundance of carefully selected words and phrases to suggest the ugliness and sordidness of the environment:

. . . in that ugly neighborhood of miserable houses, all raised on stilts or constructed with boards or sheets of zinc. Painted with loud colors, the houses were now faded and filthy. Only a foot and a half separated each one; a few leaned over toward their neighbor, as if in conversation. They were all caricaturish. The twisted lines, the broken boards, the motley array of colors, the flimsy posts, the bizarre architecture derived from cast-off material—all this turned the wretched dwellings into tragic caricatures. Just like the beggars or vagabonds whose tattered clothing once belonged to the well-to-do, so those houses were built of old and unserviceable materials from other homes in the city. Over here a cornice, over there an intricately wrought iron grating—there was something grotesque about them. Some houses had several stories, one room over another. One might say that at certain hours the worst of those houses made sinister grimaces. Overturned canoes could be seen in the streets, along the sidewalks. Here and there a willow tree, sometimes tucked in between two houses and in a line with them, appeared to be weeping over such poverty. The streets were unpaved; the ground appeared black because of the constant dampness of the earth. Dirty diners and hovels seemingly unsuitable for human beings alternated with the decent but very poor houses of the workers of the island. From all directions, the masts of ships loomed over the rooftops or the trees. And the three ferries, gigantic and black, visible from any corner of the area, overlooked that ghetto like a huge prophetic obsession. (pp.17-19)

In the manner but not with the intensity of the Naturalists, Gálvez brings in other elements of Rosalinda's disadvantageous heredity and environment. With racial bias, many self-styled patriots in the period 1880–1920 criticized the immigration policy of permitting thousands of unschooled Italians to enter Argentina. Gálvez attacks this common prejudice in presenting Rosalinda's family background. Although her father was a native Argentine, a *criollo* of many generations back, her mother was the daughter of an Italian immigrant who ran a cheap diner in a poor and sometimes violent section of Buenos Aires called La Boca. Deliberately, Gálvez further states that Rosalinda's mother was industrious and, considering her poverty and national origin, quite well educated. Her father, under the constant stupor of alcohol, came to believe that he did not sire Rosalinda. His cruel and disdainful treatment of his wife brought about her premature death when Rosalinda was two years old, after which he refused to live in La Boca because it was a "neighborhood of Italians" (p. 24).

From her window, Rosalinda looks down on El Farol Rojo, a combination of cinema and brothel frequented by sailors and loafers. The hard faces of the prostitutes, the lascivious words and gestures of the men, and the loud cries of the drunks conjure up a sinister criminal world for Rosalinda. Carnival time, too, provides scenes of vulgar sensuality:

It was sensuous music, coarse, base, a mixture of insolence and depravity, of stiffness and voluptuousness, of infinite sadness and the vulgar joys of the brothel, a type of music that spoke in slang and in the argot of prisoners, and which made one think of scenes of prostitution, of slum environments inhabited by figures of the underworld. (p. 65)

Rosalinda was brought up by Saturnina, a perverse and resentful woman whose cruelty bordered on the criminal. Saturnina's son is the degenerate El Chino, depicted in such a broad, conventional fashion as to be virtually undistinguishable from all others of his type. El Chino is just a puppet of a man, a weak fictional creation with no character of his own, although the role in which he is cast is central to the novel because of his relationship to Rosalinda. With superficial and not very convincing explanations, Gálvez writes that Rosalinda's fall stems from El Chino's almost hypnotic influence over her. She is compelled to abandon decency and self-respect and is even conditioned to accept willingly his repugnant caresses. Having lost all moral sense, she becomes his accomplice in robbery and vice. El Chino at first permits her to work in the meat-packing plant, but soon forces her into prostitution. But a ray of hope enters Rosalinda's life with the love of Daniel Forti, a young factory worker whose role in *Historia de arrabal* brings to mind that of Monsalvat in *Nacha Regules*. But Forti is as poor a novelistic creation as El Chino, and even more weakly delineated. Forti's virtuous and altruistic character contrasts sharply with El Chino's baseness. And much of the novel's appeal lies in the fact that the two men in Rosalinda's life are at opposite ends in the scale of human decency and that she is inextricably caught in a maze of conflicting emotions. On the one hand Forti inspires love, hope, and confidence; on the other, El Chino fills her with repulsion and fear. Violence abounds in the novel as an indication of the depraved environment surrounding Rosalinda: she is abused and beaten by El Chino, and on one occasion brutally attacked by a grubby English sailor. At one point in the story, Rosalinda decides to kill El Chino out of sheer desperation. Her plan is thwarted when he deftly snatches the revolver out of her hand just as she is about to pull the trigger. This scene serves as a prelude to the far more tense and dramatic one occurring at the close of the novel, when El Chino surprises Daniel and Rosalinda in the modest apartment they have just set up to mark the start of a new life together. A fight ensues and one of El Chino's henchman disarms Forti. Then, in a diabolical move, aware of his malevolent influence over her, El Chino plants a dagger in Rosalinda's hand and menacingly says to her: "Obey me, I tell you, obey me" (p. 159). All too well Rosalinda understands these words as an imperious command to kill Forti. She feels strangely impotent to disobey his order as his gaze strikes terror in her heart. For his part, the ingenuous Forti thinks that El Chino will be Rosalinda's victim and not himself. When she draws near and embraces him, little does Forti suspect that she will mortally stab him in the chest. With malevolent satisfaction, El Chino smiles and says, "She understood me, do you see? She understood me" (p. 162). Gálvez disposes of Rosalinda's emotional reaction to this horrendous act in a short paragraph which reemphasizes the cycle of deterministic forces that have shaped her life:

When Rosalinda saw Daniel Forti's dead body, she seemed to awaken from her dream. Brutal and horrible reality returned to her consciousness. It was she, who adored that man and was going to be finally free through his efforts, it was she who had murdered him. (p. 162)

III *A Man's Tragedy in Love*

Referring to *La tragedia de un hombre fuerte* (*The Tragedy of a Strong-Willed Man*), 1922, the Chilean novelist Eduardo Barrios commented: "Rarely have I read in a novel such valuable, discerning, and transcendental pages of feminine psychology." [11] An exaggerated statement from a fellow novelist, but not without its basic element of truth. Indeed, this novel contains the most extensive and perceptive treatment of love in any of Gálvez' works. Not a minute analysis of one love affair, but rather, a multipronged probing into the hearts of five women in the life of Victor Urgel.[12] And Urgel's varied emotional response to each of these women also penetrates the male psyche to a depth rarely found in our novelist. Rather arbitararily but effectively, Gálvez chose to compartmentalize various types of love: "love-imagination," "love-passion," "love-pity," "intellectual love," "the will to love." These five categories serve as the thematic background for five separate chapters, which are carefully interwoven into the rest of the narrative material. The awakening, development, and ultimate failure of each love affair constitute an independent and complete story, the only structural unit binding the narratives together being the figure of Urgel in his vain search for contentment. The tragedy of his life is the tragedy of these five adulterous affairs. Yet *La tragedia de un hombre fuerte* is more than a study of love; it is as well a social study of modern Argentina and the dichotomy between progressive Buenos Aires and the conservative provinces. The work thus treats a theme already taken up in *La maestra normal* and *La sombra del convento*. Symbol of the capital is congressman Victor Urgel; symbol of the inertia and restrictiveness of provincial Córdoba is his wife Asunción, whom readers of *La sombra del convento* recall as the daughter of austere Ignacio Belderrain. Urgel stands for the destruction of outworn values and the spirit of social unrest that presses for renovation, while Asunción incarnates the worst of the traditional forces of the past that stifle progress. Given her parochial background and emotional reserve, Asunción's marriage to Victor was bound to fail. Their opposing natures set up a barrier that compels him to look for fulfillment in other women. What Urgel seeks is an antidote to his feeling of emotional isolation and loneliness. Each new amorous attachment is no more than an attempt to escape this solitude. For the early 1920's in Latin-American fiction, this theme of inner solitude, if not entirely new, was unusual. Gálvez anticipates such writers as Eduardo Mallea and Ernesto Sábato, who penetrate this theme more profoundly and make it the focal point of their fiction. The face that Victor Urgel shows the world, the self-confident and aggressive legislator, has another more somber side that conceals more basic characteristics. Neither his conjugal life with Asunción nor the impersonality of his official position permits him to show himself as he really is, to communicate freely and genuinely. Thus the "tragedy," since Urgel, thwarted in his need to give of himself unselfishly in compatible relationships, takes refuge in adulterous love and painfully learns that it cannot bring him emotional satisfaction.

La tragedia is well conceived and thought out, but its excessive length and diffusiveness limit sustained interest and artistic unity. There is a tedious sameness in the narration of Urgel's five successive affairs which makes one very nearly run into the other. Had Gálvez reduced the number, he would have achieved a more cohesive narrative structure. Fortunately, the strongly delineated characterization of Urgel compensates for this structural weakness. Yet some critics have reacted negatively to Urgel as a fictional creation. Germán García is too harsh when he writes that "there is more pretension than reality and the strong man falls at the first analysis like the weakest puppet."[13] Alfred Coester criticizes the novel on two counts, stating that the reader does not have any interest in Urgel as a character and that "nothing is Argentine" in the work.[14] Urgel may tire the reader, but he rarely fails to interest us because we are always privy to the complex duality of his character. And Coester's second stricture seems unwarranted even if only the first two chapters are considered, in which Gálvez vividly contrasts Buenos Aires and the provinces.

The time of the novel is 1918-1922, post World War I, a period which Gálvez understood as a particularly significant one in the social revolution of Buenos Aires.[15] What he observed, rather ingenuously, was a relaxation of moral and ethical standards in every stratum of society. Relations between the sexes were more open, less controlled. External conduct was freer, mores permitted a less inhibited, less formal behavior at social gatherings, on the street, in public vehicles. In censorious tones not very different from those heard in our own times, Gálvez derided the youthful rebellion against social restraints. Youth sought to destroy traditions and parental ties that threatened to obstruct their freedom. The novelist saw the undermining of established patterns of social comportment as a factor in the deterioration of the traditional values on which Argentina had built its moral strength in the colonial period—respect for authority, religious faith, patriotism, and perhaps most essential of all, rejection of pretense and sham. To these qualities he added feminine propriety under all circumstances, implicit in which were severe restrictions in sexual behavior, dress, dancing, and smoking. Rather banal commentaries they are, but made by Gálvez with conviction and sincerity although not without a certain irritating naïveté. Into this changing social scene, he placed Victor Urgel, a man of action rather than of reflection, liberal in his political philosophy and disposed to effect his program of social reforms to the displeasure of conservative elements in the capital. Yet Urgel does not deny the values of his country's colonial past, but wants to destroy those static features that are dissonant with modern Argentina. Urgel's involvement in the many crucial issues of his day enables Gálvez to write about the influential Unión Cívica Radical, the ideologies of the Conservative and

Socialist parties, and the political machinery operating in the national senate.

The sexual freedom shown in Victor's liaisons is obviously a patent example of the moral transformation of Buenos Aires. Gálvez thought he was bold in writing so freely on love in 1922, and even affirmed that the novel contained much of Paul Bourget's *Psichologie de l'amour moderne*. In France, Gálvez asserted, his novel would not have been considered so daring.[16] Yet in his minute analysis of states of love, he is never sensuous, never even suggestive. Description of physical love or passion is totally lacking. What he succeeds well in doing is exploring the circumstances, causes, motivation, feelings, and other psychological factors involved in relationships of love. Although there is more than a little truth in the affirmation that the women are "cerebral creations of Gálvez, not observed from real life,"[17] it does not follow that this objective probing into the feminine heart lacks true meaning for the reader, or that he cannot relate to the conflicts presented. Besides, Urgel's novelist friend Eduardo Iturbide provides an alternate narrative focus to complement that of the omnipresent Gálvez. In the role of the philosophical commentator on women, Iturbide conveniently appears on the scene to speak to Victor in periods between love affairs, thus enabling Gálvez to furnish the reader with a sort of post-mortem examination of the recently terminated liaison. On one occasion, Iturbide refers to Urgel's relationship with saintly Marta Veracruz:

> We should not judge the idealism of women by those who sin. The true idealists generally do not sin. Their lack of sensuality protects them. But even many of the sinners, the most distinguished and elegant ones, prefer spiritual love, for it is more in accord with their refinement. Marta Veracruz, for example, deep down in her soul and in a moment of voluptuousness, may have desired sexual relations with you, purely for the moral pleasure, since she does not know any other. But you can be sure that she prefers the present situation. And if you had possessed her and she had enjoyed your caresses, she would still prefer to love you as she does now—with purity of feeling. (pp. 319-20)

The protagonist never enters into a frivolous affair, yet he is incapable of establishing a mutually satisfying relationship with any of his lovers. Each woman fills a different need for Victor, or he fills a need for her. The pattern followed in relating each affair is a rigid and straightforward one in which either the narrator or Iturbide serves as the all-knowing commentator. Some brief observations on three of Victor's paramours suffice to enable us to see the types of conflicts and situations presented.

For Marta, raised in the most severe moral atmosphere and forced to sacrifice her own well-being to care for her sick parents, Victor is the only person to whom she can freely pour out her emotions. Yet because of her upbringing, she feels more capable of loving like a mother or sister than like a woman. Emotional inhibition leads to physical inhibition or even fear, and although she does not lack desire she never yields to Victor.

As the prototype of "intellectual love," Elsa Brandán is in many respects the feminine counterpart of Mauricio Sandoval, protagonist of *El cántico espiritual.* Gálvez characterizes this love as "divorced from the senses, even from the heart—a plenitude of mutual understanding, of spiritual and intellectual affinity" (p. 253). Beautiful, cultured, elegant, but painfully reserved, she is unhappy in her marriage to a crass businessman. With obvious bias, Iturbide affirms that Elsa's detachment from the everyday material concerns of life makes her a rare type in Buenos Aires, although not in many artistic circles in Paris. Victor holds sufficient fascination for Elsa to become the object of this type of pure, platonic love, devoid of physical response.

Fittingly, Victor's last affair is with a woman he truly loves but who possesses no more than the will or desire to love, not the capacity to give of herself. Although Lucy does surrender to him sexually, harboring the illusion that she loves him, she cannot give him the unselfish affection he needs. After he leaves Lucy, Victor becomes despondent and doubts his own capability to find emotional fulfillment. The novel ends with his rejection of love as an important force in his life and his renewed activity as a liberal politician.

IV *The Anguish of Solitude*

The theme of emotional solitude, secondary in *La tragedia de un hombre fuerte,* becomes the predominant one in *Hombres en soledad* (*Men in Solitude*), 1938, one of Gálvez' richest novels in social content, but regrettably among the most disorderly in structure. The thematic importance of the work merits a more flexible and imaginative narrative technique than Gálvez uses in order to bring out its message most effectively and provide for the most artistically pleasing experience for the reader. It is surprising that Gálvez did not pay greater attention to formal technique in such a major novel. The plot is diffuse and lacks cohesion.[18] The many threads of narration that point to man's inner loneliness function independently as separate components, only loosely linked to each other. What the novel lacks is a clearly outlined path along which the main story line can move. There are too many points of focus, with no one single point having narrative priority over the other.

For some time Gálvez wanted to write a novel revealing the spirit of Buenos Aires in what he considered its solitude, indifference, and impersonality. He sought an appropriate manifestation of this theme and found it in the need of many *porteños* to escape their environment and live in Europe. Although spiritual loneliness, emotional retreat, and incommunicability among men are themes treated more fully by the postwar generation, 1940-1960, Gálvez felt a similar disquietude on contemplating man in the complexity of Argentine society of the 1920's and 1930's. The anguish he experienced was not as yet formalized in the term "existential," but its substance derived from the same emotional preoccupation. We have already seen that he dealt with inner solitude in portraying Victor Urgel.[19] This theme is a natural outgrowth of his interest in describing social atmosphere and depicting characters unable to adjust to their surroundings. The protagonists of many of Gálvez' novels are at odds with their environment, finding it hostile or not conducive to the fulfillment of their aspirations or way of life. Thus, Carlos Riga and Nacha Regules in Buenos Aires, José Alberto Flores in Córdoba, and even the ingenuous Raselda in La Rioja demonstrate attitudes and behavior that are essentially protests against generally expected modes of living. They retreat and are isolated; they are solitary figures in their nonconformity. Man's inner solitude in Gálvez' early novels is thus closely linked to the protagonist's inadaptability to his milieu, although it is not presented systematically as a psychic phenomenon, as in *La bahía de silencio* (*The Bay of Silence*) or *Chaves* of Eduardo Mallea, or in *El túnel* (*The Tunnel*) of Ernesto Sábato. The prototype of Gálvez' "men of solitude" is Gervasio Claraval, a lawyer by training but more interested in the arts and creative writing than in the practice of his profession. Shades of the novelist himself, no doubt. Like many *porteños,* Claraval seeks his real identity in European cultures. To mask his loneliness he longs for residence abroad, where as a foreigner he may live unencumbered by the social and cultural pressures encountered at home, while at the same time absorbing a rich intellectual experience. Surrounding Claraval is a group of malcontents who likewise flee from the banal reality of their existence, finding an escape in politics, religion, illicit love, frivolities, or extended trips to Europe. To the basic theme of inner solitude Gálvez adds secondary ones that he associates with modern Argentine society: the religious poverty of Buenos Aires, the tedium of life resulting from the mechanical, formalized behavior forced on the *porteños,* dissimulation and hypocrisy in personal relationships, arrogant pretension, and emotional isolation. Gálvez' thesis—as unoriginal as it is idealistic—is that man suffers from this inner loneliness because he rejects those spiritual elements which can counteract the pernicious effects of his utilitarian society. In choosing to live for materialistic gain and sensuous pleasure, modern man fails to cultivate higher spiritual values and engenders within himself a feeling of emptiness and futility.

Hombres en soledad is notable for its portrayal of the upper-class *porteño* of the 1920's. Censure of its frivolous and pretentious pattern of life is implicit in Gálvez' choice of characters and the situations in which they become involved. Claraval, overly idealistic, marries into the rich and socially prominent Toledo family and soon senses the impenetrable barrier between his own values and those of his wife Andrea. Financial difficulties crush his dream of residing in Paris and he soon becomes a bitter and anguished man. Unrealistically, he wants to believe that in the cultural environment of the French capital he will develop into a better and more important writer.[20] And his wife's indifference to his aspirations aggravates the marital disharmony. Andrea eventually forsakes her husband for the empty comfort of her father's home, and Gervasio in lonely desperation forms a liaison with his long-time friend Brígida, an aggressive advocate of woman's emancipation from social and sexual restraint.

As a fictional character, Claraval is interesting only because of what he represents conceptually to the reader, not because of what happens to him or what he does in the novel. Owing to the intellectualization of his character and the existential anguish he suffers, he resembles a typical creation of Eduardo Mallea. In Mallean fashion, too, he walks through the hostile streets of Buenos Aires, thinking, meditating, and above all observing humanity around him and trying to find his place in it. In Claraval's case, walking also becomes a way of lightening his emotional burden, of feeling less alone; he wants to see people, to witness the behavior of crowds, to reach out and touch the masses. But what he sees makes him further despair, for he cannot escape recognizing his own anguish in the solitude and boredom on the faces of the passersby. Gálvez describes what Claraval observes along one of the busiest and most fashionable streets of the capital:

Florida Street, at nightfall. People and more people, in constant waves, as in an uninterrupted public demonstration. Hundreds of lonely men were passing by with slow steps, or, standing on the corners, were watching others pass by. Tight-lipped men who looked eagerly, desperately, at the few women in the street. Men who did not laugh, who did not smile. If by chance they walked in two's or three's, they did not speak. They looked at the faces of those who went by. . . . Why were they surveying the crowded street from one end to another with apparent aimlessness? Why were others standing on the street corners? Almost all were white-collar workers. They had just left their offices. . . . They had spent many silent hours with papers and figures, alone with those things. And they had gone out to the street in search of another atmosphere, in search of a human emotion, of a face they knew, of the eyes of a woman who might look at them. Many of them appeared brutalized. They had a slightly frightened expression, which was also fatalistic and despairing. These men wanted to feel like men. . . . And to feel like men they went out to that street of desolation, to mix with other men, to breathe the same air, to see them pass by with the same grief, with the identical tedium.[21]

Claraval continues his stroll along the broad Avenida de Mayo, through the sidewalk cafés, where the idleness and emotional withdrawal amid apparent companionship disquiet him:

Avenida de Mayo. People along the sidewalks. Innumerable cafés, crowded with men. What were these men doing in the cafés? In some, an all-girl orchestra played tangos from the top of the platform. Static eyes fixed on the legs or the eyes of the girls. Ecstatic eyes fixed on heaven only knows what distant, forgotten or inaccessible things. Many of those men were alone, friendless, one at each table. Others met in small groups. A few played dice, checkers, or chess. One man unfolded a newspaper and read to himself or to others. They spoke little. A sentence from time to time. Something about the office, or the boss, or the next horserace. At times, very rarely, they argued. They could be seen making gestures. But then they got tired, as if that effort expended in arguing had crushed them. Claraval had known those café gatherings since he was a boy and a young employee. But it seemed to him that now there was more sadness in those gatherings, more silence, more fatalism, more loneliness. (pp.152-53)

Perhaps an even more extreme case of retreat in the face of loneliness is that of Casilda, Gervasio's sister. In part, her behavior has its roots in the moral rigidity of her father, who rarely relaxed his authoritarian rule over the family in all matters. To escape the confines of her restricted world and to chastise her father as well, Casilda has an affair with a wealthy ne'er-do-well who takes advantage of her desperate need for companionship to effect his conquest. Pitifully, she struggles to overcome her inhibitions and even tries to emulate Brígida's way of life, despite the fact that inherently she has a completely different temperament. In Casilda's story, Gálvez wants to point out the danger of releasing pent-up emotions too abruptly and impulsively. As the novel progresses we soon sense that she is one of the few characters portrayed sympathetically. Not even with Claraval can we build up a positive relationship, although he urges us to understand his plight. Gálvez is just as harsh with most of the other characters in the novel, describing them in one dimension only, as the embodiment of the social and cultural ills of modern Argentina.

Patriarch of the Claraval family is Gervasio's father, a stern and irreproachable magistrate, cut from the same cloth as Ignacio Belderrain of *La sombra del convento.* For critic Max Daireaux, the elder Claraval is "the compendium of all the prejudices and inexorable tenets of the old provincial society: rigid and narrow religion, suppression of women, disdain for artists, hostility toward the modern world." [22] His active role is slight in the novel, yet his sharply defined type—the self-righteous defender of traditional moral values—appears juxtaposed with the many characters who represent more liberal views on Argentine society. Gervasio is clearly his father's antagonist, but although he invites social change, he is too involved in his own personal conflicts to take an active role in any movement. In his mistrust of the new Argentine culture that rejects the need to emulate Europe, Gervasio seems more timid than prudent. Among other reasons, he is attracted to Europe to compensate for his lack of emotional and intellectual fulfillment in Buenos Aires; he fails to understand that most people look toward their own environment to satisfy their cultural needs. To speak for the values of a modern Argentina, Gálvez creates the figure of Pedro Roig, a novelist with an abiding faith in his country's future, in its capacity to build a progressive and prosperous society. But Argentines must know themselves, states Roig, and recognize their own deficiencies. And inner solitude may be the first step in this process of self-awareness. Quite clearly, Gálvez himself is speaking through Roig, who discerns a clear relationship between the personal anguish of solitude and Argentina's stoic recognition of its imperfections. Gálvez' position is not unlike that taken by Eduardo Mallea a few years later in *La bahía de silencio.* The central figures in that novel, all defeated in life's struggles and equally disillusioned but not without hope, have reached a sort of plateau, a temporary haven that Mallea calls a "bay of silence," from which they will soon emerge victorious and fulfilled. The words of the protagonist Martín Tregua echo Roig's thoughts:

"You and all of them have reached that place at which the angry sea of persecution and adversity licks in vain. All of you, and who knows how many others in this world, have reached the bay, that place of waiting, where their silence is concentrating and where their fruit is ripening without fear of storm or gale. How deep and beautiful is the bay! There wait those who have turned their failure into triumph. At this hour the bay of silence holds you and them. I see you all there, silent and expectant." [23]

The Toledo family provides some of the most interesting character portrayals of *Hombres en soledad*. The patriarch is Ezequiel Toledo, wealthy, mundane, and dissolute. He seeks no more out of life than the satisfaction of his sensual and material needs, and his debased values of life have left their imprint on his children. The daughter Andrea is an arrogant and sophisticated woman concerned only with practical values, while the son Bebé is a culturally pretentious youth who acts as the spoiled darling of an influential family. Although an attorney, Bebé's main interest in life is to indulge himself in the pleasures of high living. His residence in Europe had no other purpose than leisure and self-gratification. He is false to himself and to Argentina because he seeks social recognition and success without real effort or merit. Another Toledo daughter, Flavia, caters as much to her own pleasures as does her brother Bebé to his. Flavia's social position as the wife of a wealthy lawyer, Albano Loira, along with her family prestige, compels her to play the role of a culturally enlightened person, when in reality her interests and temperament are far removed from intellectual or artistic pursuits. Flavia's affectation seems to complement her husband's fawning behavior in his professional and social relationships. An opportunist and an unscrupulously ambitious attorney, Loira appears, among all the other unsympathetic characters in the novel, particularly insufferable to Gálvez. Ezequiel's brother Melchor is no less a man of the world, an influential politician who sees life as a series of maneuvers to gain the most advantageous position. Yet like Gervasio, he too is a lonely man, who hides his solitude under a facade of vanity and elegance. And he feeds his ego by having affairs with women of easy virtue, as if needing to fill the emotional void in his life by any possible means.

One other minor character deserves mention, Martín Block, whose idealism seems extreme even to so unmaterialistic a person as his close friend Gervasio. Block takes his own life when the September Revolution of 1930 headed by General Uriburu fails to achieve its avowed purposes and goals. Optimistically, Gálvez himself believed that the flaunted ideologies of this revolution could readily cure such Argentine ills as the oligarchy, the temporal power of the Church, concentrated wealth, materialism, and underpopulation. Block's suicide, the only one in Gálvez' twenty-nine novels, is the ultimate expression of the writer's disillusion over the results of the September Revolution.

V *The Fever of Horse Racing*

One work, *La pampa y su pasión* (*Horse Racing Fever*), 1926, appears totally out of step with the rest of Gálvez' literary production. He strayed far from the traveled road to portray the frenzied passion for horse racing in Buenos Aires. Many critics feel that he erred in trying to depict a social milieu alien to his interests and temperament;[24] the result could be no more than an artificial and wooden narrative. Although *La pampa y su pasión* is not among Gálvez' better works, the accusation of artificiality is too severe. The novel's weakness lies not in the portrayal of the protagonist or the physical environment, but rather in Gálvez' failure to bring to life the many secondary personages whose character and actions are central to the development of fictional interest. As if to anticipate the critics' charge of unfamiliarity with his subject matter, the novelist says that he gained the necessary understanding and knowledge by visiting the *Hipódromo* and several racing clubs and by interviewing jockeys. Thus, for the first and only time Gálvez had to go through a period of studying his subject, while in all other novels he drew on direct experience or observation. Although no comparison is suggested with the masterly depiction of environment in *La maestra normal* or *El mal metafísico*, *La pampa y su pasión* presents a believable and interesting atmosphere through a good character study of the protagonist Fermín Contreras and through descriptions of things associated with the turf: racing lore, the training of jockeys, betting, the spectators, the intrigue. Some of this material is incidental, but most of it is adroitly integrated into the novel. There is, for example, a brief account of a certain General Nicasio Ortiz, an octogenarian who fought to conquer the pampa and regain it from the gaucho. Ortiz, who has a mania for collecting items relating to horse racing, on one occasion accompanies the wealthy Federico Wilkinson to a large estate called Las Lagunas. The description of the train ride through the open pampa is excellent, although conventional, revealing Gálvez' artistic sensitivity to Argentina's most distinctive physical feature.

Gálvez neither defends nor condemns the excessive interest of the *porteño* in horse racing, but views it as an uncontrollable passion, almost as a deterministic force that snares even the most strong-willed. Betting and its financial entanglements are an acceptable evil that society has to bear. Racing even provides an outlet, claims Gálvez, for suppressed emotions that may find relief in other, more reprehensible ways. Besides, Gálvez interprets the great attraction of horse racing as a cultural phenomenon with its roots in "the spirit of the pampa which is latent in the cosmopolitan soul of Buenos Aires." [25] The statement holds a modicum of truth, but it is too exaggerated to be taken seriously. Yet the novelist romantically persists in this illusion, even suggesting that Contreras' passion for racing and his fierce loyalty to the sport bear an affinity to the gaucho's concern for his horse and his dependence on it.

The novel traces the struggle of a dedicated jockey to maintain his professional and personal integrity in the face of unscrupulous companions, an unfaithful wife, and a vengeful woman. Physically unattractive, ignorant, and socially inept, Contreras is happiest in his role as trainer and star jockey in the employ of Federico Wilkinson. Contreras' coarse wife Albertina, linked amorously with Wilkinson, sets in motion a chain of incidents that makes the jockey's upright character stand out amid the dishonesty and baseness all around him. Although Contreras knows of his wife's infidelity, he prefers to look the other way out of weakness and a strange sense of professional loyalty even to the man who dishonors his home. In her role as the socially emancipated woman, frivolous and opportunistic, Albertina is cast in the same mold as Flavia and Brígida in *Hombres en soledad.* Perhaps a more abhorrent character is Indiana Reyes, Wilkinson's former lover whom he gives up for Albertina. Although her part in the story is significant, Indiana is only faintly drawn. She attempts to ruin Wilkinson by devising dishonest schemes at the race track and even tries to enlist Contreras' help. But the jockey values his honor more than he does personal revenge and refuses to lose a race deliberately to betray Wilkinson. Contreras eventually breaks down under the strain of his domestic and professional conflicts, neglecting himself physically, disregarding training rules, entering into illicit relationships with women, frequenting bars and cabarets, in short castigating himself to bring attention to his plight. The character portrayal of Contreras is not only one of the novel's strongest features; it is perhaps superior to the novel itself. In not developing the figure of Wilkinson, philandering, hypocritical, and base, Gálvez lost an opportunity to create a strong character in opposition to Contreras. Despite the strength that derives from the Contreras-Wilkinson association, the depiction of Wilkinson remains superficial and inert, merely a cold symbol of the parasitic forces that all too commonly control racing.

CHAPTER 6

The Novel and History

G ALVEZ' passion for history overflowed into the historical novel. His strong views on his country's past and a tendency to consider issues and people in terms of a formal sequence of events led to much more than a passing interest in that type of novel. Like all novelists he wanted to approach his historical fiction first as literature and then as history. But in some cases the result belied his intent. While in the three novels on the Paraguayan War Gálvez' narrative skill prevents history from overwhelming the fictional element, in the Rosas series history becomes the dominant ingredient at the expense of literary and artistic values. The Paraguayan War novels easily pass as good historical fiction; the novels on the Rosas era are no more than mediocre works. The former series was published at the height of Gálvez career and greatly enhanced his reputation; the latter series, save for the first two, came out in the twilight of his career and added little to it. It is with this unevenness of literary worth that we consider these two groups of novels.

Gálvez claims no literary influences on his historical novels, in particular on *Escenas de la Guerra del Paraguay*. In truth, there were few Argentine writers of historical fiction to emulate. It is doubtful that nineteenth-century works such as José Mármol's *Amalia*, 1851, or Vicente Fidel López' *La novia del hereje* (*The Sweetheart of the Heretic*), 1855, with their cloyingly sentimental tones, could have served as a model for Gálvez. Nor does he give the slightest indication in his voluminous memoirs that he even read historical fiction from other Latin-American countries. He does remark[1] that at the time he wrote *Escenas de la Guerra del Paraguay* he had read a few of the *Episodios nacionales* of Galdós. He admired Tolstoi's *War and Peace*, but states that it could not serve as his guide. Finally, as if to anticipate those who might mention Sir Walter Scott as a possible influence, he comments that he never read a word of the Scottish novelist. What is clear is that, even though there may be no direct influences on his historical fiction,

Gálvez exhibits in these works the same type of conventional objective realism that characterizes his social and psychological novels. As far as technique and style are concerned, his historical works fully complement his other fiction.[2]

I *A Fanatical Paraguayan Dictator*

The three novels on the Paraguayan War form a well-defined thematic and artistic unit, although each one is independent of the other as regards plot and characters.[3] The trilogy ranks high on the list of Gálvez' literary achievements, and not a few critics have proclaimed it his masterpiece.[4] *Las escenas de la Guerra del Paraguay* is a graphic reconstruction of an apparently unequal struggle during the years 1865-1870: Paraguay on one side and the triumvirate of Argentina, Brazil, and Uruguay on the other. Paraguay was obviously outnumbered, but the fanaticism of dictator Francisco Solano López and the fierce patriotism of the troops and civilian population prolonged the conflict for five years. Paraguay was totally crushed, with a large percentage of her male population either killed or incapacitated. "A civil war," Gálvez calls the conflict, as if to underscore the tragedy of one small nation fighting three larger and more powerful neighbors. The immediate cause of the conflict sprang from Argentina's refusal to allow Paraguayan troops to cross her territory to attack Brazil and Uruguay, with whom Paraguay was already at war. But more fundamental reasons involved geographical, political, and commercial rivalries that served as a constant source of tension and resentment. The Paraguayan War was the culmination of deeply rooted animosities among the four nations struggling to liberate themselves from dictatorship or anarchy and attain political and economic sovereignty.

Gálvez is the omnipresent narrator of the events in the three volumes of the series, but his vantage point is different in each of them. In *Los caminos de la muerte* (*The Roads of Death*), 1928, the conflict is seen mostly from the Argentine battlefield in and around the province of Corrientes; in *Humaitá*, 1929, the focus of interest is the heroism of the Brazilians; while in *Jornadas de agonía* (*Marches of Agony*), 1929, the enfeebled Paraguayan troops are cast in the central position. The three novels describe distinct phases of the war. *Los caminos de la muerte* treats the first months when the combined forces of Argentina, Uruguay, and Brazil march north toward Corrientes, driving López from Argentine territory. In *Humaitá* the allied armies push on to reach Paraguay, contending with a hostile physical environment as well as the enemy's bullets. Their reward is the surrender of the Paraguayan fort which gives title to the novel. In *Jornadas de agonía* the capitulation of the Paraguayan capital Asunción serves as the focal point of the novel, while López' death after his insanely protracted resistance hastens the end of the gory conflict.

Each of the novels has a similar narrative structure—a direct, orderly, chronologically sequential presentation of the course of the war, set against a background of several families whose lives are inextricably drawn into the struggle. The war is thus considered in more than its military aspect. It is seen not as some distant, impersonal conflict between soldier-symbols, but as a conflict involving men whom the reader knows as husband, brother, father, friend, in short as human beings in personal relationships. The device of tying in domestic entanglements with military operations is a felicitous one. It not only provides for a broader-based perspective of the war, but also supplies the essential fictional ingredient in each novel, the imaginative element that gives literary value to the portrayal of historical events. The many descriptive passages which such a large canvas allows contain fine examples of Gálvez' prose at its best.[5] With equal skill, the novelist paints the clashing of armies, the suffering of the troops, the hardships imposed on the civilian population, the grieving of a soldier's loved one, or the savage madness of Francisco Solano López. Note the following description of the physical difficulties encountered by the Argentine soldiers in their march toward Corrientes:

That march from the Ayuy camp toward the north, begun on July 18, was becoming an intolerable torture for Antonio and all the front-line troops. Few winters as cruel as that one. Every two days, if not more often, terrible storms hurtled down on the camp. The hurricane uprooted the tents, and shook them violently, and the soldiers in the murky night, half-naked and trembling in the cold, were at the mercy of the storm. The camps were turned into muddy lakes and the Uruguay River, which they were skirting, became a sea. In their march, the troops had to tread through the mud or contend with water up to their waists. The frost made the storms even worse. Many nights there was no wood to rekindle the fires extinguished by the strong winds, or the wet wood would not light. Several men died of cold. They went to bed in good health, although weakened by fatigue and poor food, and by morning they were dead. And they made these frightful marches barefoot, their pants rolled up to the knees, their feet and legs punished by the thorns and stones in the road.[6]

*   *   *

The descriptive vigor of *Los caminos de la muerte*[7] is what first strikes our attention, as we await the gradual unfolding of plot. Gálvez sets the scene well: semi-colonial Buenos Aires, haughty, smug, complacent, almost oblivious to the problems of the rest of the nation. In that capital live the Guevaras, one of two families whose fortunes during the war comprise the fictional element of the novel. The portrayal of this rich and socially prominent family contains Gálvez' not uncommon blend of realism and subtle idealized romanticism. The Guevaras have two sons and two daughters, all of whom figure importantly either in the domestic involvements of plot or in the conflict of loyalties that arises as the war becomes more intense. The other family, the Taboadas, from the northern city of Corrientes, is socially inferior to the Guevaras but likewise financially comfortable. As the war begins, Antonio Guevara, an enlisted soldier, is forced to leave his bride of a few hours to march toward Corrientes. Antonio's sister Florinda is married to an uncouth army lieutenant, Jerónimo del Cerro, whom Rudecindo Taboada generously shelters in his home after the officer is wounded in battle. While recuperating, Del Cerro unsuccessfully attempts to seduce Señora Taboada, who, despite the affront, facilitates his escape from Corrientes. By an ironic turn of fate, Del Cerro later meets Rudecindo and boastfully lies about his conquest of a beautiful woman from Corrientes. Rudecindo foolishly suspects his wife and murders her.

There are many other incidents involving the interplay of the two families, such as the affair between one of Guevara's sons and Rudecindo's sister. In fact, Gálvez contrives so many turns of plot and personal entanglements that he fails to single out any one protagonist to bind together the related but independent parts of the narrative. Because of his appearance in several significant episodes, Del Cerro is the only person in *Los caminos de la muerte* who can be considered the central figure, but Gálvez' low-keyed subdued portrayal of the officer dissipates the impact of his frequent presence in the novel. Rudecindo, although well drawn as a loyal patriot and valiant soldier, has too limited a role to emerge as a principal figure, although Gálvez takes pains to describe his character and create dramatic situations to reveal it. The real protagonist, the Argentine critic Ernesto Palacio suggests,[8] is the "national spirit" of Argentina, a vague but evocative concept that Gálvez abundantly illustrates throughout the novel. What he tries to portray in *Los caminos de la muerte* is more than patriotism, more than national sovereignty, more than oneness under stress. It is essentially the feeling of being Argentine, of being uniquely Argentine. In the years following the Rosas dictatorship, from 1852 to 1870, the bitter dissension between Buenos Aires and the interior provinces threatened to create an irreparable rift in the nation. Gálvez felt that the national spirit was put to the test in the Paraguayan War, as troops from Buenos Aires battled Paraguayan forces in the remote province of Corrientes. Palacio is correct in saying that the thematic unity of the novel is the "goal of triumph," which can only be achieved by having all Argentines join forces and abandon their sectional differences. This seems to be Gálvez' message.

At the close of *Los caminos de la muerte,* Gálvez describes the scene in Corrientes as Argentine troops leave that liberated city and head for Paraguayan territory. In this passage, realistic detail blends with lyricism and emotional exaltation to bring out the feverish excitement occasioned by the victorious Argentine armies:

The cannon shots from the ironclads began their destruction. There, on the Paraguayan coast, huge clouds of sand were raised. Two hundred ships broke the serenity of the vast river. The sounds of reveille stirred the air, the groves, men's hearts. The Uruguayan, Brazilian, and Argentine national anthems were sung in several places along the coast and on board the ships. The cheers tried to compete with the cannon volleys and the music. And a magnificent sun, the sun of Corrientes, glorified the landscape and the heroic scene. Fifteen thousand men were departing. Coveys of white doves—the good-bye handerchiefs—waved in the hands of many onlookers.

Itapirú furiously bombarded the ships. From Marshal López' entrenched encampment, the cannon tried to sink the rafts loaded with men. The eyes of the leaders who watched the spectacle from the coast of Corrientes opened up wide with anxious expectancy. The eyes of some became cloudy with patriotic emotion. And on the cliff, before all his men, as if forming a museum picture, as if posing before History, the generalísimo watched the ships depart. The sharpness of his gaze, always calm and firm, stood out from beneath the black denseness of his beard. He stood erect and motionless, and one could say that his entire soul was concentrated in his eyes. It appeared that the sun was trying to remain on the border of his kepi, on the embroidery of his shoulders and sleeves. And just when he removed his cap to salute those who were setting out toward Death, the sun planted a long and glorious kiss on his forehead. (p. 206)

*   *   *

Of the three novels in the series, *Humaitá* is the most loosely knit. The fictional part has too many strands that tend to weaken the overall structure of the work. Lacking is a central narrative thread that the reader can follow with interest from one end of the complicated narrative quilt to the other. What Gálvez succeeds in doing so well, however, despite the diffuseness of the story line, is to create a vivid group of characters living under the suspicions, fears, agony, and strife that war imposes on the military as well as the civilian population. Even more than the other novels of the trilogy, *Humaitá* suffuses the fervor of life into the fictional environment and the characters. But this environment is seen less as a composite canvas of humanity than as life histories of individual people and families.

Just as in *Los caminos de la muerte,* the main story in *Humaitá* centers on the tribulations of a family caught up in the misery of war. Tragedy struck early in the Cienfuegos household of Asunción when the father was summarily executed for speaking his mind concerning the futility of the war and the inevitable decimation of the Paraguayan forces. Several other members find themselves painfully torn by conflicting loyalties. Character analysis and motivation become, in effect, explanations of political partisanship or domestic discord brought about by the exigencies of war and civil strife. Two of the Cienfuegos daughters consider López an oppressive tyrant, while another, married to a Paraguayan officer, idolizes her country's fanatical ruler. Of more fictional interest are the divergent paths that the four Cienfuegos brothers follow during the war. Although dissimilar, their lives show the same stresses resulting from conditions in war-torn Paraguay. The youngest son Pedro enters the army at thirteen. Eusebio, after performing heroic military service even though he personally disapproves of the dictator's policies, becomes secretary to the infamous Padre Maíz, sadistic tool of López' inhumanity against rebellious Paraguayans. Perhaps the most tragic set of circumstances involves Gerardo, who defects to the allies after a long struggle of conscience, knowing the terrible punishment that may be inflicted on his family in retaliation. And Justo, fanatically loyal to López, has no less a struggle of conscience when he makes a decision to kill his traitorous brother Gerardo.

But if the multiple folds of plot only moderately excite our interest, the many historical accounts and descriptive passages integrated into the novel furnish some of its most notable pages. On one occasion, the two opposing generals, Francisco Solano López and Bartolomé Mitre, meet to explore the possibilities for a peaceful settlement of the

conflict. The tension and sense of historic mission are well brought out
in the brief scene that describes their encounter:

There was silence. Then Mitre spoke of the treaty among Brazil,
Argentina, and Uruguay. Somberly, General López listened, suspecting
the final words. He was right. Mitre thought a moment and then said
with a quivering voice:

"The three nations that comprise the Triple Alliance would start
peace negotiations under one condition."

The General looked at him fiercely. A storm of wrath wracked his
countenance. Imperturbable, Mitre affirmed that for the good of all
López should resign and go to Europe.

The General's eyes turned red with fury. Once again his pupils
strangely dilated. Any other man but Mitre would have trembled with
fear. Did that extraordinary serenity derive from his sense of right and
reason—the supreme force? Or perhaps from the greatness of his
religious spirit . . . which placed him above men and material
things . . . ?

When López observed his interlocutor's noble and calm bearing, he
restrained his ire and responded:

"In other words, my decision to relinquish my position and go into
exile is what you propose as a condition for peace."
"That is correct."

And then . . . his lips quivering with anger and his fist clenched, he
uttered these astounding words, which the facts of history—his heroic
resistance in twenty unequal battles and his death—would later make
sublime:

"Only over my dead body, in the confines of Paraguay, shall they
impose those conditions on me."

Mitre waited a moment. The burning lava of the volcano was
extinguished in the serene waters of his spirit. And when López began
to calm down, he said:

"So there is no possible settlement. The Treaty of The Triple
Alliance . . . states that the war is not against Paraguay, but against
you. . . ."

"If that is so," declared López, also steadfast and serene, with the
serenity of anticipatory heroism, "I shall die with my people." [9]

Mitre's calm intelligence and leadership obviously impressed Gálvez,
and on other occasions in *Humaitá* the Argentine general appears on the
field of battle giving orders to his men.[10] López too is seen on the

battleground after General José E. Díaz leads the Paraguayan troops to the decisive victory at Curupaytí. Gálvez as narrator thus observes the armies of both sides as a sort of war correspondent. At one point, he watches the dreaded cholera, like a silent insidious foe, invade the Paraguayan and allied military camps:

The doctors foretold a sudden and voracious epidemic. And it happened. In just a few days, the sickness shook the tents and huts with horror. From the living quarters came moans of pain, anguished shouts asking for water, prayers. The streets separating the rows of tents became lanes for stretcher bearers. Nauseous smells fouled the atmosphere. Nobody slept, because of the groans of the sick and out of fear of contagion. Horrible news came from Curuzú, where the troops from Porto Alegre were encamping. Fifty men were busy just digging graves to bury the bodies. Many Brazilian officers succumbed. In Tuyutí the epidemic was not killing with as much fury, but the sick could be counted by the thousands. The military leaders feared the Paraguayan attack. They did not understand how López did not profit by the allied misfortune on those hopeless days at the end of April and the beginning of May. (p. 114)

* * *

The agony referred to in *Jornadas de agonía* is that of General López himself and the Paraguayan people who were forced to endure his fanaticism. As the last in the series, the novel reaffirms Gálvez' admiration for the Paraguayan masses and his strong censure of López. More than the other works of the trilogy, *Jornadas de agonía* endeared Gálvez to Brazilians by paying just tribute to her soldiers and extolling the leaders who directed the military campaign against López. Relying very heavily on precise descriptive detail, the novel depicts the bitter last stages of the war—the allied victories at Caraguatá and Peribuey and the death of López. The plot is the weakest element of the work, containing much the same format and even the same basic ingredients as the earlier novels in the series. The situations and conflicts are obviously different, the names change, yet the reader feels he has already trodden upon this fictional territory, that he is familiar with it. Two strands of plot may be mentioned: one revolves around the Rosales family of Asunción, suspected by the dictator of being disloyal and forced to flee to the forests of northern Paraguay; the other concerns a Brazilian army captain Damasceno Fragoso, who fears for his wife's safety in Asunción.

Since López lurks in the background of each novel in the trilogy, if not emerging occasionally as a live figure with active participation in the narrative, Gálvez' own feelings toward the tyrant are important to consider. Although *Los caminos de la muerte* and *Humaitá* suggest Gálvez' views, it is in *Jornadas de agonía,* and especially in those episodes centering on the dictator's last days, that the novelist affirms his position most clearly. Although he unhesitatingly justifies Rosas' iron rule, he is unwilling to do the same with the tyranny of López. His despotic regime cannot be defended on any grounds; it was immoral, unnecessary, without any economic or political reason. Yet despite Gálvez' condemnation of López. *Las escenas de la Guerra del Paraguay* pictures him with an awe of majestic heroism, as an almost legendary figure of arrogant nationalism. For the novelist he was unmercifully cruel, perverse, and diabolic, but at the same time he played the role of a great patriot and the most uncompromising defender of Paraguayan sovereignty. Particularly in those last months of combat so well described in *Jornadas de agonía,* López is portrayed as deranged and insatiable. Sheer courage in the face of overwhelming military odds and an indomitable will are two of the dictator's personal qualities that Gálvez exalts throughout the series as virtues misdirected for iniquitous purposes.

II   *The Iron Rule of Rosas*

As Juan Manuel de Rosas' biographer, although a biased one, Gálvez makes a significant contribution to the study of Argentine history. But as a novelist of the Rosas regime, he contributes little to Argentine literature or to his own reputation. *Escenas de la época de Rosas* (*Scenes from the Rosas Era*), a seven-volume series, is dull, tedious, and static. It suffers from a lack of narrative interest and a surfeit of historical detail that is not artistically assimilated into the fictional element. Not that Gálvez fails to display his technical skill and descriptive force; indeed there are many well-executed scenes and expressive narrative passages depicting the political and social climate during the Rosas tyranny. But the novels read too often like chronicles. They are heavy, overburdened with historical and political matters that are more an intrusion upon the reader's enjoyment than welcomed background material of real interest.

The first novel of the series, *El gaucho de Los Cerrillos* (*The Gaucho of the Cerrillos*), 1931, is a minute account of Rosas' early years in Buenos Aires as an aggressive political figure who eventually became the country's supreme leader. The work approaches biographical fiction, since much of the narrative material centers on Rosas himself or on the political maneuvering involved in his ascendancy to power. The period covered is from May, 1828, to December, 1829, when Rosas became governor of the province of Buenos Aires. For Gálvez, Rosas' arrival in the Argentine capital put an end to a ten-year period of anarchy and ushered in an era of peace and order. The novelist makes no effort to restrain his enthusiasm and admiration for the tyrant. There is deliberate irony in the final scene describing the funeral of the executed Federalist governor Manuel Dorrego and the welcoming of the new official, Juan Manuel de Rosas. The elaborate funeral, the spectacle, the excitement, and the rush of people apparently make the fallen leader the center of interest; yet Gálvez makes us feel in the background the more important presence of Rosas, anxiously awaiting the termination of this final reminder of his predecessor and anticipating his own rule as well.

Like the novels of the Paraguayan War, *El gaucho de Los Cerrillos* utilizes family conflicts and feuds as the basic fictional element. What is brought out clearly in this novel is that opposing political views frequently cause estrangement and even open hostility between once friendly families. Gálvez sets up numerous cross-relationships among members of the Hinojoso family, staunch Federalists, and the Montellanos, equally fervent Unitarian partisans. Not satisfied with a passive political role, Tomás Hinojoso seeks personal revenge on the Unitarians, and in particular on the arrogant Lieutenant Montellano, for whom he harbors uncontrollable animosity. The love story between the children of the rival families—Tomasito Hinojoso and Remedios Montellano—is trite and weakly presented. In the characterization of one of the Hinojoso sons, José Rafael, as a deceitful, hypocritical, and cowardly person, Gálvez vents his own enmity against the Unitarians. Yet despite his bias, the novelist can also portray sympathetically the plight of the Unitarians as the vanquished faction in a divided Buenos Aires. Julián Montellano, after a series of personal and political misfortunes, feels that his world has collapsed. Stripped of his material possessions by the victorious Federalists, angered by his daughter's affair with an Hinojoso, and distressed over his son's indifference, he turns to religion for his only solace. Buenos Aires he can no longer endure, and along with thousands of other Unitarians flees to Montevideo in search of a new life.

When the second novel in the Rosas series came out in 1932, the Argentine press paid little attention to it, but it won the National Prize in literature for that year. The protagonist of *El General Quiroga* is the same "tiger of the llanos" that Sarmiento portrayed so venomously in his *Facundo* of 1845, but Gálvez paints a favorable picture of him as a popular hero. As a provincial political boss, Quiroga was suspected of rivalling Rosas for supreme command in Argentina. The novel covers the years 1830-1837, a period when Rosas' power became firmly established and unquestioned. The opening pages describe Quiroga's arrival in the capital amid the cheers of the populace, despite the fact that he has just suffered a minor defeat at Oncativo at the hands of the Unitarian General José M. Paz. Ostensibly, Rosas plays host to Quiroga, but in reality becomes his jailer, ordering his henchmen to spy on his movements and conversations. Outside the limits of his own provincial territory, Quiroga wields no power. At the close of the work, during the masquerade ball, news of Quiroga's assassination spreads quickly. Significantly, this novel and the preceding one end with the elimination of two men who might have prevented Rosas from gaining complete control of his country. The fictional element is too pat and un-developed to be in the least convincing. Suffice it to say that Gálvez prefers to focus attention on one family, the Lanzas of Buenos Aires, whose members hold so markedly diverse political views as to form a microcosm of a divided nation.

The five remaining novels of the Rosas series, written after a lapse of sixteen years, cover events from 1835 to the dictator's defeat at Caseros in 1852. The relatively tranquil period from 1835 to 1839 is described in *La ciudad pintada de rojo* (*The City Painted Red*), 1948, which takes its title from the truculent measures adopted by Rosas to maintain his iron rule. The simple plot involving the breakup of a *porteño* family because of conflicting political beliefs is commonplace, lifeless, and at times naïvely sentimental. The action, what there is of it, is extremely slow. Emotional feeling and behavior, more often than not, are motivated by purely political reasons. At this point in the series, the third novel, the reader begins to weary of the similarity of situations and the sameness of Gálvez' stock characters: a bereaved father who sees disunity in his home, a daughter whose suitor or husband is aligned with the political foe, distrust and rivalry among brothers. In *La ciudad pintada de rojo*, Gálvez' portrait of Rosas is less political, far more human and spontaneous than in the other works of the series, as if the novelist were desperately searching for a way to gain the reader's sympathy for the dictator. Besides Rosas, several well-known historical personages appear in the narrative, but they play no active role. With that romantic emotionalism which he not infrequently exhibits, Gálvez has one of the characters, Rita Claustro, fall in love with the Argentine poet Esteban Echeverría, even though she has never met him. More meaningfully, he intersperses commentaries about such national figures as Pedro de Angelis, historian, propagandist, and advisor to Rosas, Estanislao López, Federalist *caudillo* of Santa Fe, and Juan María Gutiérrez, poet and Argentina's first literary critic.

In *Tiempo de odio y de angustia (Time of Hatred and Anguish)*, 1951, the principal focus is on the Unitarian leader Juan Lavalle during the years 1839-1840.[11] Particularly important in this novel is Gálvez' impassioned defense of Argentine sovereignty against the threat of French intervention. Lavalle and his supporters, Gálvez tells us, would have sold out to the French or would have granted them economic concessions unfavorable to the nation's best interests. In *Tiempo de odio,* Gálvez again lashes out at the Unitarians through manipulation of plot. It is narrated that a band of Unitarian youths raped the widow of a loyal Federalist; Ursula Jardony is the daughter born of this attack. When she grows to womanhood, her two half-brothers, unaware of the true relationship, vie with each other for her affection. Finally, Ursula's mother reveals the secret. One son, the worthless Bonifacio, almost kills one of Ursula's many suitors, but an epileptic seizure prevents him from doing so. The fifth novel in the Rosas series, *Han tocado a degüello (The Slaughter Begins)*, 1951, treats of civil strife in the interior and northern provinces from 1840-1842. It was a period of confusion and terror for the citizens of those regions engaged in a conflict they knew would ultimately be resolved in distant Buenos Aires. Gálvez believed Lavalle was responsible for the assassination of the Federalist leader, Manuel Dorrego, which touched off the civil war. The hatred that consumed Federalists and Unitarians spread through every corner of Argentina and exploded at the slightest provocation. This tension is what Gálvez succeeds in depicting so cogently in *Han tocado a degüello,* notwithstanding the diffusiveness of the action. The story itself is among the more interesting in the Rosas series and even includes an element of suspense, noticeably lacking in most of his historical fiction. Political dissension has disunited the family of Federalist partisan Juan Pablo Laín. His son Florencio is a rabid Unitarian, an undisciplined and surly youth who, despite his faults of character, is his mother's favorite. A domestic row with his father provokes Florencio to leave home to join Lavalle's forces. Shortly after, his mother expresses a dying wish to see her son once again. As a dutiful husband, Juan Pablo sets out in pursuit of Florencio despite the risk of entering the Unitarian camp. This search is a felicitous narrative device that fills many pages with suspenseful action and provides a counterbalance to the cold historical material. When Juan Pablo fails to track down Florencio, he sends his younger son Conejo to continue the search. But the Unitarians discover him and shoot him as a spy. Apprised of his brother's execution, Florencio breaks his allegiance to the Unitarian cause and, after a series of incidents, returns home and reconciles his differences with his father.

The siege of Montevideo and the complex question of Argentine-Uruguayan relations are treated in full detail in *Bajo la garra anglo-francesa* (*Under the Anglo-French Claws*), 1953. The novel is written in the guise of the memoirs of a fictitious adventurer, a certain Prudente Wells, a wordly, cultured person with important political connections. Wells is portrayed as a man-about-town who earns his living as a moneylender. He lives a frivolous private life and a dangerous political one as a Unitarian partisan in Montevideo. To abet the Unitarian cause he even agrees to pose as a Federalist at great personal risk. Much of the novel centers on Wells's amorous and political adventures in El Cerrito. Particularly well defined is his affair with a servant girl, Cleofe, whom Gálvez considers the best realized female character in the Rosas series.[12] *Y así cayó don Juan Manuel* (*The Fall of Don Juan Manuel*), 1954, ends the Rosas series, and Gálvez' defense of the dictator is as fervent as in his first novel. The work relates the last years of the regime and the dictator's defeat in 1852 at the hands of General Justo J. de Urquiza. The plot is the most uninspired and shallow in the series. Yet the historical events are carefully developed and are all the more compelling to the reader since they deal with the end of one era in Argentine history and the beginning of another.

The novels of the Rosas era can stand no comparison with those of the *Escenas de la Guerra del Paraguay*. From every artistic standpoint, the Rosas series is inferior, in basic fictional interest, in narrative vigor, and in verbal expression. It was far too ambitiously conceived, even for an exclusively Argentine public; seven dense novels portraying a thirty-year dictatorial rule cannot avoid becoming cumbersome and tedious even in the hands of the most gifted author.

III *The English Invasions of 1806 and 1807*

Understandably, Gálvez undertook to write of still another chapter in his nation's history: the English invasions of 1806 and 1807.[13] Even though these events generate less emotional and far less political reaction than the Rosas regime or the Paraguayan War, they played a significant role in Argentina's emergence from a Spanish colony to an independent republic. In 1806, although the political bonds had not yet been severed from the mother country, England took advantage of Spain's weakened condition at home and in America to attempt to colonize Argentina. That the attempt was frustrated is in part a tribute to the people's sense of *argentinidad* even prior to independence from Spain. The victory over the British helped to give Argentines the resoluteness and confidence to overthrow the Spanish regime a few years later. Yet, as Gálvez points out in the novel *La muerte en las calles* (*Death in the Streets*), 1949, a small faction supported the English invasions as a way of avenging the abuses and injustices perpetrated by the Spanish masters. With his usual precision and detail, Gálvez documents the historical events and portrays the important leaders of the day—Liniers, Sobremonte, Alzaga. One of the novel's notable features is the depiction of the social and political climate in Buenos Aires in the late colonial period. And presented just as vigorously is the hour-by-hour account of the preparations, strategy, and actual fighting between the English and Spanish forces. There follows, by way of example, one such description:

July 5, 1807 arrived, a Sunday. At six-thirty, when the shadows of the night still covered the city, the English soldiers proclaimed the attack with twenty-one cannon shots. From the defenders' forward positions, situated in Plaza Nueva, three rockets quickly announced the British advance. The fortress answered with three abrupt cannon shots to warn the populace. Drums sounded in the streets and bells rang. The people were bewildered and frightened; for the first time they heard an enemy's artillery. And the murmur of women praying was heard over the reverberating, precise sounds of the musketry. (p. 340)

Quite naturally, the fictional element in *La muerte en las calles* involves the interrelationships that develop among the English soldiers, the Spanish forces, and the Argentine civilians. The central figure is Sergeant Pedro Lunabril, who falls in love with the daughter of Toletino Azcárate, rabid patriot and stern father. The story takes on added interest when a young English officer, Richard Burns, attracts the attention of Azcárate's wife Goya. One night, as Goya is entertaining Burns in her bedroom, her husband spies them from afar. Suspecting that it is his daughter Jimena and not his wife who dares defile the sanctity of his home, Azcárate forces her to marry the English soldier against her will. All of these somewhat contrived and artless lines of plot are unfolded against a methodically constructed background of military operations. The story continues as Lunabril plans to kill Burns to avenge Jimena's honor. Burns is only wounded and after his recovery is sent away to a prisoner of war camp during the second invasion of Buenos Aires. At the same time, Goya becomes jealous of her daughter's apparent love for the Englishman. Through an anonymous letter sent by an envious relative, Azcárate learns of his wife's adultery and orders her to commit suicide or leave the city. Fate intervenes in this uninspired story when she is subsequently killed in an accident. In the closing months of the second invasion, Burns again heads his detachment and is fatally wounded by Lunabril and an accomplice. The work ends with Lunabril and Jimena offering each other eternal vows of devotion and love in an atmosphere as falsely romantic and unconvincing as the novel as a whole.

CHAPTER 7

Biography as Historical Interpretation

FROM the writing of historical novels to the writing of biography may be just a short step. Gálvez' abiding interest in Argentine history led him to study the lives of several leaders who shaped the destiny of their country, for better or for worse.[1] The success of *Escenas de la Guerra del Paraguay* proved that his passion for history could be channeled into fiction. Many parts of his next two historical novels, *El gaucho de Los Cerrillos* and *El General Quiroga* resemble pure biography in their presentation of the lives of Rosas and Quiroga. When Gálvez abandoned the Rosas series in 1932, he turned to biography and the following year published his first work in that genre, *Vida de Fray Mamerto Esquiú.* Gálvez was disappointed in the public's tepid response, but far from discouraged. From 1934 to 1938, he returned to the novel, publishing two minor works and the very significant *Hombres en soledad.*

But then a change; for the next ten years he wrote no fiction, but became totally absorbed in biography. For Gálvez, that genre was a natural extension of his fiction.[2] Because of his interest in psychological motivation and the interplay of character and environment, he thought of biography as more than the mere recording of the external facts in a man's life. It should carefully assess the subject's actions, scrutinize his moral and social conduct in public and private affairs, above all weigh the impact of his life on his contemporaries. Gálvez used biography to divulge history and interpret it in the light of his own political beliefs and ideological values. His was not a casual venture into biography; he wanted to reexamine many areas of Argentine history and reappraise his country's leaders. Although not a professional historian or academician, he felt that certain periods in Latin-American history were poorly recorded or not recorded at all. His biographies, then, would fill these gaps and correct errors in historical analysis. Two qualities stand out in these works: a personal, impassioned view of his subject; and a striking but at times excessive accumulation of descriptive detail and data of all kinds. The strength of his biographies of Juan Manuel de Rosas, Domingo F. Sarmiento, and Hipólito Yrigoyen lies precisely in these qualities. Gálvez takes a strong and frequently unpopular stand on these and other figures, utilizing all manner of dialectic to convince the reader of his position. The fact that he can be controversial and dogmatic creates added interest in the biographies. And the massive array of information he assembles, coupled with sustained enthusiasm in presenting it, is his most effective means of supporting his points of view. He overwhelms us with his thoroughness, and although we may not be persuaded we are always impressed.

Of the nine biographies, seven deal with Argentines, one with an Ecuadorian, and one with a Colombian. To classify the subjects another way: five—and the five most significant ones—were leading political figures of Latin America; one an important poet; one an influential churchman; one a gaucho *caudillo* or chieftain; and one an obscure seminary student. Four of the five statesmen lived in the nineteenth century, while one was the biographer's contemporary. Gálvez' view of biography as personal history more than as a literary genre is reflected in the dominance of political subjects. His ardent religious dedication is seen in his choice of Fray Mamerto Esquiú and Ceferino Namuncurá as subjects and in his laudatory treatment of Gabriel García Moreno, Ecuadorian dictator and fanatical defender of Catholicism. An obvious intent, too, lies behind the selection of the other subjects. Each one reveals a corner of Gálvez' feelings, beliefs, and ideas, in short the dynamics of his life. In writing of the lives of others, he found an effective outlet for the expression of his own philosophy and ideology.

I *A Priest in Córdoba*

Chronologically, *Vida de Fray Mamerto Esquiú,* 1933, stands apart; it is the only biography written in a period when Gálvez' principal interest was in the novel. All the others belong to what we may call his "period of biography," from 1939-1948. *Esquiú* is the most artistically written of the nine biographical works, containing beautiful descriptive passages of the sleepy, isolated city of Catamarca, the subject's birthplace. Gálvez' skill as a writer of fiction shows through in his technique as biographer, for he portrays Esquiú's environment with as much care as he would in a novel. The biography depicts an unselfish life devoted to God and humanity. Gálvez follows the thoughts and deeds of Esquiú (1826-1883), beginning with his days as a young priest acclaimed for his sacred oratory and his courageous denunciation of

Spanish rule. In 1881 he became Bishop of Córdoba, that bulwark of colonial tradition and austere Catholicism. In the graphic descriptions of Córdoba, Gálvez the biographer again takes a lesson from Gálvez the novelist. Interestingly, Ignacio Belderrain's Córdoba in *La sombra del convento* and Esquiú's Córdoba are one and the same; yet in the novel Gálvez attacks the city's religious conservatism and severity, while in the biography he sets his focus on the beauty and serenity of its spiritual atmosphere.

II *Hero and Anti-hero*

Of far greater importance than the Esquiú biography is *Vida de Hipólito Yrigoyen,* published in 1939. As the leader of the *Partido Radical* or Liberal Party and president of Argentina from 1916-1922 and from 1928-1930, Yrigoyen dominated the political scene for nearly two decades. His name conjures up the intrigue and maneuvering of national politics, and the charisma surrounding his person continues to attract historians. For the masses, the poor, the working class, Yrigoyen (1852-1933) was a hero; for the rich, the privileged, the oligarchy, he was a betrayer. Although Gálvez strongly defended Yrigoyen, he considered him a "man of mystery," as the subtitle of the work indicates. Of all his biographies, he found this one the most difficult to write, in part because Yrigoyen was an astutely silent and withdrawn man who spoke of himself but rarely. The paucity of personal correspondence written by Yrigoyen or directed to him compounded the difficulty. If the public knew the man's deeds, it did not know the man. Behind the facade he presented to the public was an enigmatic figure with deep personal conflicts and anxieties. Gálvez probes for explanations of his external conduct. He recognizes that his subject's complexity lends itself to the same kind of character analysis used in his novels.[3] As biographer, Gálvez seems to be wistfully recalling his years as a creative writer of fiction when he remarks that "in Yrigoyen's life is present all that attracted me as a novelist: the multitudes, the picturesque, the tumultuous, the human, the Argentine." [4]

Throughout the biography, Gálvez points out that Yrigoyen was a product of the peculiar Argentine social and political system that owed little either to the United States or to Europe. Gálvez admits there may be disagreement concerning Yrigoyen's social liberalism, but his chauvinistic spirit of *argentinidad* is never questioned. His neutrality in World War I was the single most divisive issue of his presidency. Gálvez heartily applauds his position and praises his courage in the face of worldwide opposition. More significantly, Gálvez considers Yrigoyen the defender of Argentine economic independence against the encroachments of England and the United States.

Yrigoyen lived for politics; it dominated his every act and thought to the point of fanaticism. He was austere, disciplined, and the first Argentine president to "invoke God, Divine Providence, and the Gospels in his official documents" (I, 305). With Gálvez' strong religious feeling, he felt he had to pass moral judgment on Yrigoyen, asserting that he was an upright, honest leader, a true Christian but not a practicing Catholic. He describes him physically as well, and notes how he talks and acts. And some passages adroitly fuse physical characteristics with mental and emotional qualities. Yrigoyen's bearing and physical presence attract Gálvez:

His figure produces an impression not only of patriarchal calmness and serenity, but also of greatness, of augustness. He generates such enormous respect around his person that no one dares argue with him, doubt his words, or request him to explain them, or even set forth an opinion contrary to his. . . . (I, 193)

At the close of the biography, after relating the circumstances surrounding Yrigoyen's defeat by General Uriburu in 1930, Gálvez expresses compassion for a great humanitarian who was betrayed by his own Liberal Party and even by the proletariat. The revolution that overthrew him, Gálvez laments, meant a step backward in social reform and a return to power of the privileged classes and the indifferent bourgeoisie.

III *Again Juan Manuel de Rosas*

Gálvez' next biography, published in 1940, raised a storm of controversy because it defended the dictatorship of Rosas (1793-1877). Only two of the Rosas novels had appeared when Gálvez started this work, in which he affirmed even more directly and personally his unpopular support of the tyrant. *Vida de don Juan Manuel de Rosas* reveals the same painstaking research as *Hipólito Yrigoyen,* but a far greater bias freely admitted by Gálvez in the preface. The Rosas era, he states, was clouded in ignorance, misinformation, and prejudice until the appearance of his biography. In fact, he acknowledges that he himself was an *antirrosista* in his youth, simply because most of his teachers and all his textbooks denounced him. What urged him to think more favorably of Rosas was his revaluation of the Unitarians, whom he came to consider as an aristocratic and intellectual group that looked more to Europe than to Argentina for its cultural and political views. As Gálvez' opposition to the Unitarian cause increased, his sympathies turned toward the Federalists and their leader Rosas. Through assiduous research in newspapers and archives, the whole story of the era unfolded to him in unequivocal terms. His conclusion: Rosas was an indisputable benefactor to Argentina. By 1928, when his first Rosas novel appeared, he was an uncompromising Rosas partisan, contending that an iron hand had been necessary to preserve Argentina's sovereignty and that the Federalist leader represented the conscience and spirit of Argentina.

Democracy and liberty seem to be muddled concepts in Gálvez' mind as he is forced to provide an explanation for Rosas' nefarious deeds:

> Many people think that Rosas, as a dictator and even as a "tyrant," was not a supporter of democracy. This is an error. Democracy means "government of the people," with liberty or without it, for that really does not matter. There is no doubt that Rosas governed with the consent of the people and represented the people. And finally, dictatorship can be a means of attaining political and social democracy. (II, 436)

The Rosas biography complements the Rosas novels, but is an even more determined effort to vindicate the repressive regime by focusing more intensely on the dictator himself. For Gálvez, there is no question that the end justifies the means. His argument is that Rosas ruled in abnormal times, when all governments are despotic or at least have to resort to harsh means to control the country. Rosas' dictatorship was justifiable because it was expedient, unified the nation, and prevented it from succumbing to the economic and political pressures of the French and English. Argentines should be grateful to Rosas for his accomplishments and understand his tyranny as the price they paid for them. For the majority who disagrees with Gálvez, these palliative statements of his are completely unreasonable and painfully ironic.[5]

IV *The Schoolmaster President*

In *Vida de Sarmiento,* 1945, Gálvez again takes an unpopular stand, this time attacking one of his country's most distinguished statesmen and educators (1811-1888). The biography is an imposing work of investigation and documentation, but its intent, unfortunately, is to stain the image of the "schoolmaster president," as Sarmiento is frequently called. Not that Gálvez denies his importance in Argentina's material development, nor his fame as a civic leader. But he berates Sarmiento at every turn—his egocentric and aggressive personality, his political ideology, his ethical and social conduct. Boldly, Gálvez questions his achievements in his role as progressive legislator and liberal leader and even raises doubts about his universally recognized contribution to education, remarking that "the entire educational program during his presidency should be credited exclusively to Avellaneda" (II, 951). The public, the critics, and the press censored Gálvez for trying to tear down the flag that had flown so gloriously over Sarmiento's head for so many years. Many book dealers were unwilling to exhibit the Sarmiento biography in their showcases, and some even refused to sell it. But basic interest in the great patriot and the attraction of Gálvez' name were sufficient to assure the book a modest commercial success.

Sarmiento was an archenemy of Rosas and vented his hatred in his celebrated book *Facundo,* 1845. For Sarmiento, the element of *barbarie* (barbarism) in Argentina was the gaucho and the *caudillo* (regional political and military boss), and the physical environment which nurtured them played a decisive role in shaping their way of life. Facundo Quiroga and Rosas typified this *barbarie,* while Buenos Aires and its culture represented the element of *civilización,* progress, and education. Gálvez recognizes the literary merits of *Facundo,* its human warmth, its passion and descriptive color. But his antipathy toward those who attacked Rosas caused him to say that as a work of history *Facundo* is a "collection of lies" (II, 699). Neither does Sarmiento's book of reminiscences, *Recuerdos de provincia* (*Recollections of Provincial Life*), escape Gálvez' criticism, for he charges him with writing "two hundred pages and genealogical tree to tell us about himself, his relatives, and even his servants" (II, 797).

Gálvez portrays Sarmiento as an extreme egotist, an arrogant and arbitrary man who stepped on innocent toes to attain his goals. Very little that Sarmiento did as governor of San Juan province or as president of the nation made a favorable impression on Gálvez. He accuses him of allowing Buenos Aires to acquire excessive power and of nulligying the gains made during the Rosas era to attain provincial sovereignty. Querulously, he even assails him for continuing the Paraguayan War out of spite, out of personal hatred for dictator López. Nor can he resist denouncing Sarmiento's attitude toward religion and the Church. While conceding that the statesman was not wholly indifferent to spiritual needs, he finds fault with his pragmatic concept of religion and his anticlerical views. Resorting to hyperbole, Gálvez at one point states that "everything Catholic inspires Sarmiento with horror" (I, 1076). He sees in him the very antithesis of the logical, reasoning, and disciplined man that the term *civilización* implies. In part Gálvez is correct, yet he fails to recognize that this very impetuosity and unbridled imagination is one of Sarmiento's most valuable qualities. He seems to forget that Sarmiento was a typical Romantic writer, that he defended the new current of romanticism against those who denied literature its freedom of expression and form. Gálvez regrets that instinct and improvisation rather than careful meditation rule him, that strong will rather than calm intelligence drives him. Gálvez wrote an informative and passionate biography, but most Argentines lament that his enthusiasm and attention to detail were not matched by a greater appreciation of Sarmiento's qualities as political leader and educator.

*   *   *

Any assessment of Gálvez' importance as a writer must include his biographies. They form an integral part of his literary production and not merely a peripheral chapter. Indeed, many readers know only one Gálvez—the biographer of Rosas, Sarmiento, and Yrigoyen. Just as much as his novels, Gálvez' biographical works reveal him as a fervent nationalist, with a particular brand of nationalism that cherishes law and order above individual freedom, that seeks to preserve at any cost a rigid and narrow concept of national sovereignty. His most important biographies were written to expound his nationalistic views: the basic role of the Catholic Church in maintaining the essence of the Argentine spirit; the seeking of Argentina's cultural heritage not only in the colonial world, but also in Spain itself; mild distrust of Anglo-Saxon civilizations; and grave doubts about the value of a totally democratic government. The verbally combative spirit that Gálvez keeps under control in his novels emerges with released energy in his biographies. And whether these biographies are polemic, like *Rosas,* placid like *El santito de la tolderia* (*The Young Saint of the Indian Camp*), or religiously oriented like *Esquiú,* they complement his fictional writing to a marked degree.

CHAPTER 8

Gálvez on Morals and Religion

A^T this point, we must be well acquainted with Gálvez' religious devotion and fervent defense of the Catholic faith. In *La sombra del convento* his Catholicism rejects dogmatism and intolerance, even when used in support of Catholic beliefs. In *La maestra normal* he suggests that a sense of religion might have prevented Raselda's fall; that is, lacking spiritual faith she was less able to resist sin. With greater ardor than that of any other Latin-American novelist, Gálvez touches on man's religious experience in many of his novels and utilizes it as the central theme in several other works: *Miércoles Santo* (*Holy Wednesday*), 1930; *La noche toca a su fin* (*Night Draws to a Close*), 1935; and *Perdido en su noche* (*Lost in His Darkness*), 1958. In all three novels, his position is not unlike that of the preacher offering examples of the consolation and rewards of dedication to God. Gálvez' moral and didactic purpose is as manifest in these works as is his hope for social reform in his thesis novels. The interplay of environment and character, so essential an element in the earlier works that established his reputation, is relegated to a secondary position in these novels. Instead, he directs our attention toward ethical and spiritual values that assumed an increasingly significant role in his life. His sense of religious duty, his concern for moral issues, and his interest in the spiritual nature of man may seem incompatible with the themes of lasciviousness, prostitution, drunkenness, and violence that abound in the novels of his early period. Actually, no such incompatibility exists. We recall the scandal that *La maestra normal* caused. Many timid critics were shocked by Gálvez' choice of subject matter and his attention to earthy details in descriptive passages. When assailed for these realistic touches, he responded defensively that no one should object to what he wrote since his inoffensive treatment of sin and vice clearly revealed his high moral and ethical principles. In short, Gálvez does not wish to flaunt his realism. He is caught between his sense of moral righteousness and his need to draw a faithful picture of life.

I   *Torments of a Father Confessor*

By far the most important of Gálvez' novels of religious or moral theme is *Miércoles Santo,* which has enjoyed wide popularity in Hispanic America and, through translation, has reached German, French, English, Italian, and Czech readers. The work is brief, compact, direct, exceedingly simple in narrative structure. The protagonist is Father Eudosio Solanas, austere if not ascetic, but with an uncommon understanding of the human heart. Interest in the novel centers on the problems of those who seek his counsel and consolation and on the inner conflicts of the priest himself. What strikes the reader's attention at the outset is the ironic parallelism between the anguish of Father Solanas and the weaknesses and vices of the people he spiritually comforts. The irony of the consoler himself in need of help forms an interesting base for the religious and psychological study of the troubled Father. And when through fortuitous circumstances his personal torment and the suffering of a penitent he is confessing become interrelated, the irony becomes emotionally charged and highly dramatic. His agony is that as a novitiate he nearly succumbed to the temptations of a young woman enamored of him. Now, as a priest, he doubts he is without carnal desire. Old memories haunt him as he performs his religious duties that Holy Wednesday. He even feels tempted by Satan and on one occasion takes a penitent doubter for the devil himself.

Sinners of all kinds come before him, including an adulteress and an unwed mother seeking an abortion. To all he listens attentively, superb in his dual role as confidant and moral judge, yet fearful that he himself may fall victim to man's natural instincts. One American critic notes that "the asceticism of his life, his fasting and self-flagellation, were a means of subduing this evil of the flesh." [1] By chance, the last person to appear before the Father is the same woman who tempted him many years ago. She feels ashamed because of many illicit liaisons she formed in subconscious retaliation for his rejection of her advances that fateful day. Torn between hatred and love for him, the girl confesses to Father Solanas her emotional ambivalence, obviously not aware of the identity of her confessor. When the priest recognizes her voice, he also recognizes his own weakness as a man. When he hears from the woman's trembling lips "Now ... I hate him. But if I met him ... I think I should pursue him to make him love me" (pp. 168-69), he fears that Satan has finally vanquished him. The emotional strain proves too overwhelming, and he even imagines that the black figure of a man has suddenly turned into a monster with a human face and wings of a bat. His physical strength gives way and he dies convulsively before the image of the Virgin.

The psychological probing into the mind and heart of Father Solanas and his penitents is the most noteworthy element of *Miércoles Santo*. A venal judge coming before the priest, for example, provokes these words:

Father Solanas stayed silent for a moment, shaking his head and letting inarticulate sounds issue from his mouth. These sounds were sketches of exclamations, bits of words bitten off by his jaws before they could get out, hieroglyphics of thought which Charity prevented from taking further shape.

Because he loathed this sin, or anything like it. Here there was not the excuse of human weakness. Carnal sins, however grave, however sad they might be, had at least some explanation. Man carried them inside himself. He was like a lion tamer in a cage, and it was easy for one of the beasts to escape.

But the sin of this penitent, committed in cold blood, scarcely deserved pardon. The carnal sinner was often an unfortunate man who might have a good foundation of morality. Corruption, aggravated by years of contumacy in it, presupposed a character profoundly debased. The penitent's social position increased the ugliness of his sin still more. (p.144)

II *A Sculptor and Platonic Love*

The idealism of such characters as Monsalvat and Riga reaches its extreme expression in the figure of Mauricio Sandoval, protagonist of *El cántico espiritual* (*The Spiritual Hymn*), 1923. Idealism was not a pose for Gálvez. As a young man he expressed it as a romantic, quixotic longing for social betterment; as he matured intellectually, he showed it in his rejection of the materialistic values of Buenos Aires society. In *El cántico espiritual* the sculptor Mauricio is a disoriented and frustrated young man who vainly seeks ideal conditions for the cultivation of his art. Society can neither accommodate him by meeting his unrealistic needs, nor can he compromise his ideals to fit into society. This aspect of idealism is not new in Gálvez, but in Mauricio's case it is developed around a platonic relationship with a married woman. The lack of emphasis on the two environmental settings, Buenos Aires and Paris, seems deliberate on Gálvez' part, since the novel illustrates an aesthetic position rather than a social or moral one. Indeed, the theme of platonic love is in harmony with Mauricio's search for that undefined value that Gálvez calls "absolute beauty," pure and unsullied.

El cántico espiritual stands apart in Gálvez' fiction because of its static, overly expository mode of narration. There is less action and movement, less dialogue, and above all less direct involvement with real issues of life than in any other work. Monsalvat and Riga are visionaries too, but their idealism is set in a clearly defined, readily identifiable environment that acts as a counterbalance. Mauricio's idealism is not seen beyond the confines of his own constricted world and therefore meets little counterthrust to engage the reader's attention. Spiritual and idealistic values certainly form part of the total vision of man; in *El cántico espiritual,* regrettably, these values constitute the predominant element.

III   *A Sinner Redeemed*

No religious event moved Gálvez more than the International Eucharistic Congress held in Buenos Aires in October, 1934. The Congress brought added fervor to his religious devotion and prompted him to write the short novel *La noche toca a su fin*, 1935. The story concerns a sinner's repentance and conversion through the inspiration of the Congress. Claudio Vidamor has led a dissolute and evil life, to a large measure, Gálvez says, because of his lack of religious training as a child. What is more, Vidamor was not even baptized, owing to the objections of his domineering father, a Freemason and opponent of Catholic doctrine. As a journalist in Buenos Aires, Vidamor can conveniently expound his misanthropic views, viciously attacking religion, priests, and orthodox morality. The characterization of Vidamor is the stereotype of an immoral scoundrel and is far too pat to have much artistic or novelistic appeal. It is as if Gálvez accused him of every conceivable vice and villainy, only to present him at the close of the novel as a spiritually regenerated man.

Gálvez was very conscious of narrative technique in *La noche toca a su fin* and tried two new devices: the alternation of first- and third-person discourse, and the use of a written confession as narrative material. In Chapter I, set in italics, Gálvez tells us that a certain Claudio Vidamor is excitedly at work putting down on paper his sordid biography and the extraordinary events that have just altered the course of his life. What follows is Vidamor's story from infancy to the day, some forty-two years later, that he accepts Catholicism after witnessing the Eucharistic Congress. Intercalated in this main narration are six brief sections, also in italics, that introduce each part of Vidamor's story and contain as well moral and psychological comments on his aberrant way of life. These six interpolations serve a double purpose: they break up the long first-person narrative into several smaller, more manageable episodes; and they help to form a bond between Vidamor and the reader, with Gálvez serving as intermediator.

The description of events at the Congress is the most vivid part of the novel. Gálvez is at his best when he describes the excitement and religious zeal of the masses as they witness the pageant. Depicted with his usual precision and color are the huge processions along the Avenida de Mayo, the stirring discourses of the clergymen, the chanting of hymns, the populace's mixed emotions of joy, awe, and sublimity, the rush to kneel and confess and receive Communion. As the Congress progresses, Vidamor is drawn into its exuberance, first as a sinner, then as a penitent. His initial expression of scorn for the Congress reaffirms his journalistic invectives against the Church. An impassioned radio sermon, however, deeply touches Vidamor's heart, and he soon loses all will to resist the call of religion.

IV *Adultery and Atonement*

The theme of adultery, one of many transgressions treated in *Miércoles Santo* and *La noche toca a su fin,* occupies Gálvez' full attention in *Cautiverio (Captivity)*, 1935, a work which the author himself values more for its moral significance than for its artistic qualities.[2] The novel relates episodes in the adulterous life of María Elena Larrandy and her ultimate redemption and marital reconciliation. Like other novels of Gálvez, *Cautiverio* provoked the indignation of many critics who thought it aroused carnal desire and even glorified illicit affairs. As in the case of *Miércoles Santo,* the author felt compelled to defend his position, stating that in his portrayal of María Elena he censures adultery and never describes or even suggests sexual relations. This is true; he depicts an unhappy, tortured woman, and not once goes beyond the bedroom door. Directly related to his denial of treating sin too openly is the image he again wishes to project as a Catholic novelist, as one who protects the cardinal principles of the faith and portrays his characters in terms of their acceptance or rejection of those precepts. He conceives of *Cautiverio* as a struggle between man's sexual passion and his need to control it. As the title indicates, man finds himself a prisoner of his own baser instincts, frequently without the will to conquer them. More significantly, Gálvez treats concupiscence as a deterministic force that shapes man's existence. María Elena is the captive, the victim of an inexorable desire or need to engage in extramarital affairs. But if in her the novelist wants us to see the modern woman in a modern, emancipated society, he has mistaken the extreme for the norm. While the devil has tempted María Elena too frequently, her husband, socially and morally conservative almost to a fault, seems inspired and controlled by the virtues of the saints. The antithetical nature of husband and wife is too contrived and exaggerated, but the analysis of character traits in both cases is penetrating, fitting in well with Gálvez' moral and religious preoccupation with virtue and vice.

Gálvez is little concerned with environment in *Cautiverio*. The physical milieu of Buenos Aires is caught only fleetingly, although many references to its social mores are made in the novel. The frivolous leisure class to which María Elena gains entrance because of her husband's position as a judge is the object of Gálvez' censure. Juan Larrandy is an antifeminist, opposing women's recently-acquired social rights. He decries smoking, public exhibitions of dancing, the reading of realistic novels, and the wearing of cosmetics. Ironically, he eventually grants his wife permission to engage in these innocuous activities, while he feels no need to get at the root of her infidelities.

V   *The Doubts of a Jesuit Priest*

It is fitting that Gálvez' last two novels again demonstrate how intensely engrossed he was in religious matters. *Perdido en su noche* appeared in 1958 and *La locura de ser santo* (*The Madness of Being Saintly*),[3] written the same year, was published posthumously in 1968. The central figure in *Perdido en su noche* is a young Jesuit who abandons the Order shortly after taking his final vows. Gálvez' sensitive handling of this delicate theme of apostasy reveals his ability to treat the difficult interrelationships between religious devotion and the dictates of conscience. Had he published the novel in the 1930's, along with *Miércoles Santo* and *La noche toca a su fin*, it might have had greater success than it did. But in 1958 Gálvez' traditional, lineal technique of fiction was not in vogue, the critics and public favoring a more involuted treatment of even the most simple and common themes.

Perdido en su noche is the only novel Gálvez wrote that takes place in his childhood home of Santa Fe, but he does little to make us feel the provincial setting. With only a few scattered references to that city, the work lacks a thematically significant milieu. Its real environment is the spiritual, moral, and emotional world of Teodoro Troncoso, whose intense struggle within himself transcends any ambience. The development of Teodoro's complex character is carefully examined and his ultimate decision to renounce the Order is not discordant with the emotions and states of mind he displays throughout the novel. We see Teodoro first as a boy of fourteen, the son of a devout but domineering and selfish mother.[4] In a moment of extreme spiritual fervor, as her husband lies gravely ill, she vows to have Teodoro enter the Jesuit Order. Although unsuited by temperament for a religious life and disinclined to follow the rigid discipline of the Jesuits, the boy goes off to Córdoba to begin his training. Doubts and misgivings about his vocation beset the young seminarian at every turn. Even his effort at writing for the Jesuit journal are frustrated when an article of his on the "dangerous" subject of Freud is rejected. Above all, he questions his ability to be a patient and prudent teacher and spiritual counselor in the Jesuit tradition.

In having Teodoro's mother dictate the career her son is to follow, with all the disastrous consequences, Gálvez is protesting the selfish ends for which religious devotion may be used. Indirectly, *Perdido en su noche* also represents an indictment of religious authoritarianism and pedagogical inflexibility, which under any guise can only encourage hypocrisy and sham. Once ordained, domestic complications add to Teodoro's problems. Anguished, tormented, and confused, Teodoro sees no other answer but to abandon the Order, a decision as difficult as it is terrifying. Hatred and scorn soon descend on him from all sides; his mother, brother, and neighborhood friends all condemn his action without showing the slightest understanding. The only person who now accepts Teodoro is a good-natured servant girl whom he marries despite her family's objections. In many respects her relationship to Teodoro is another example of Gálvez' penchant for romantic idealization, analogous to the Nacha-Monsalvat liaison or even the Lita-Riga friendship in *El mal metafísico*. In all these cases, the disparity in social class or education between man and woman is offset by a bond of mutual need and sympathy.

The peace of mind Teodoro gains in marriage does not endure, for pangs of guilt and spiritual emptiness begin to beset him. Feeling the need to accept God again, to repent and be saved, he kneels before an altar in a burst of religious ardor and utters: "Why, my Lord, did I abandon You? I must have been mad. In truth I never ceased to believe in You or to love You" (p. 238). Considering himself unworthy of being in God's presence, Teodoro staggers out of the church and into the path of an automobile. His violent death is thus made all the more dramatic by his spiritual rededication only a few moments before. The pure and simple devotion to God ultimately professed by Teodoro matches the genuineness and emotional simplicity of his love for the servant girl. The basic message of *Perdido en su noche,* written in the mellow tranquility and religious preoccupation of Gálvez' later years, involves a trust in the goodness of God in the face of today's dispassionate relationships.

* * *

Gálvez erred in thinking that the category "Catholic novelist" would confer on him special literary recognition. His unstinting efforts to inculcate in Argentines a feeling of spirituality and devotion to the Church are admirable. But the well-deserved fame he earned for these efforts resulted far more from his essays, biographical writings, poetry, and the example of his own life than from his fiction. Indeed, had he not written any religiously oriented novels, his reputation as a staunch defender of the Catholic faith would in no way suffer. As literature, his best religious or moralistic fiction possesses many other artistic qualities to recommend it besides the expression of man's spiritual nature. Thus, *Miércoles Santo* is more significant for its human values than for its religious ones; *La sombra del convento* presents a comprehensive view of colonial Córdoba that transcends the religious conflict that tortures José Alberto Flores. And the basic defect of his weaker religious novels, such as *La noche toca a su fin,* is that the purely spiritual or moral themes cannot support the demands of interesting fiction. Although Gálvez may feel his religion deeply, he is more adept at depicting social environment and psychological conflict than in portraying man's spiritual being.

CHAPTER 9

The Closing Novels of a Long Career

IN 1954, when he finished the last novel of the Rosas series, Gálvez was seventy-two years old, with a long and fruitful career behind him. Most novelists would have laid down their pens and proudly glanced backward at their accomplishments. Not so Gálvez, who even at that advanced age looked ahead to writing more novels and even revising some old ones. From 1954 until his death in 1962, he finished six novels, in addition to his memoirs, a slim book of verses, and a volume of essays.[1] The significance of these novels pales before that of his earlier fiction. They favored his reputation only in the sense that his name was thereby kept alive to a new and different generation of readers and critics. They certainly failed to enhance his literary stature. And not a few critics and friends would have advised him to stop novel writing after the completion of the Rosas series. Be that as it may, these novels were not totally ignored. They appeared in the show windows of Buenos Aires book stores; they were reviewed, although not extensively, in newspapers and magazines in Argentina and other Latin-American countries; and they form a revealing closing chapter to his literary career. The six novels of this group are the following: *Las dos vidas del pobre Napoleón* (*The Two Lives of Poor Napoleon*), 1954; *El uno y la multitud* (*One and the Multitude*), 1955; *Tránsito Guzmán*, 1956; *Me mataron entre todos* (*Together, They Killed Me*), 1962; *Perdido en su noche*, 1958, and *la locura de ser santo*, 1968. For reasons of thematic unity the last two have already been treated in the previous chapter on Gálvez' religious and moral works.

I Two Lives in One

The first novel of this later period, *Las dos vidas del pobre Napoleón*, is interesting if only because it breaks completely with Gálvez' reliance on objective realism. The novelist calls the work a "literary caprice," as if to counterbalance the somber Rosas novels that immediately preceded it. The tone of *Las dos vidas* is frequently light, sometimes whimsical, with social background playing a negligible role in contrast to most of Gálvez' other works that rest heavily on environmental-psychological conflicts, religious and moral issues, or historical setting. In this work Gálvez spins the fanciful story of a modest, unassuming middle-aged man who decides to lead a frivolous and daring life in imitation of a character in a novel he has just read. Napoleón Machuca sees in this fictional character, Alejandro Magno Pacheco, the reckless and carefree man he secretly longs to be. So fully does Napoleón become immersed in Alejandro's character that he gradually loses the ability to distinguish his own being from that of his fictional counterpart. The two identities, the one fictional and the other real, merge and blend in the confused mind of Napoleón. His mental disorder leads the reader to ponder such questions as whether Alejandro is really Napoleón's conscience, or his true self, or his baser instincts, or whether together they form one being. In admiration, Napoleón models his own behavior on the unconventional ways of his idol and alter ego. He becomes involved in all sorts of difficulties both at home and at work, engages in extramarital affairs, commits fraud with the assistance of his employer's wife, and winds up the deranged victim of his own imagination.

In *Las dos vidas,* Gálvez deals with a complex psychological theme, but fails to develop its full potential for novelistic portrayal. The story is shallow and too simply and at times naïvely narrated to bring out the full import of the subject matter treated. In no other novel do his directness of narration, undeviating course of plot, and unadorned prose turn to disadvantage. Its weighty theme demands a more sturdy plot, a more interrelated set of conditions and circumstances surrounding the protagonist, and a more sophisticated prose style. In a word, the novel runs on too thin a rail. For the first time, Gálvez abandons his strict observance of realism and explores the world of the subconscious and the imaginative. The undercurrent of whimsy and mock seriousness does not obscure the novel's principal intent to inquire into the meaning of human existence. In *Las dos vidas,* the psychological probing present in many of Gálvez' other works reaches the farthest recesses of man's mind and extends to the realm of the speculative and the unknown.

* * *

In *Me mataron entre todos,* Gálvez continued his interest in the metaphysical and the subconscious. Like *Las dos vidas del pobre Napoleón,* the novel centers on a strange case of mental aberration. The protagonist is Segismundo Cuenca, professor of philosophy, who suddenly acquires the ability to read the thoughts of others, to divine their intimate feelings. This intuitive faculty soon causes Segismundo untold embarrassment and emotional stress. Like Napoleón, the professor is sufficiently rational to recognize his own aberrant condition, but helpless to constrain it. Yet unlike Napoleón's illness, which psychiatry can explain and even understand, Segismundo's case lies beyond the realm of accepted scientific knowledge or theory. The problem of personal identity which troubles Napoleón also haunts Segismundo, who questions the reality of his own existence and even considers his life as just a horrible dream.

II *Argentina and World War II*

Argentina's controversial position in World War II forms the background of *El uno y la multitud,* a novel of social and political ideas in which Gálvez again speaks out on many problems affecting his country. The work is more a platform for the exposition of political doctrine than a sustained piece of creative fiction. The title refers to the painful anonymity of the *porteños,* those millions of inhabitants of Buenos Aires who seem to lose their real identity in the impersonal and competitive metropolis. The difficult years from 1941-1947 brought Argentina into direct contact with the ideologies of nazism, fascism, and communism. On the one hand, Argentines were caught up in the welter of international politics; on the other, they were overly concerned about nationalism and economic sovereignty. A supporter of Argentine neutrality, Gálvez feared British and American economic imperialism, but was oblivious to the threat of German intervention. No less significant an issue raised by Gálvez in *El uno y la multitud* is the abandonment of rural areas in favor of the more economically promising capital. Buenos Aires was beckoning thousands who sought a better life, but absorbed them only physically, for they were never fully received into the mainstream of life in the capital.

The novel is in part a sequel to *Hombres en soledad,*[2] for it continues the life of Gervasio Claraval in his struggle to adjust to Argentine society. But he suffers a radical change in ideology as the later novel unfolds; and the portrayal of that change is one of the most interesting features of the work. Claraval, who has always deprecated the values of Argentine culture when compared to those of Europe, comes to understand the unique heritage and traditions of his country. And the same Claraval, who in *Hombres en soledad* felt little need for spiritual devotion, finds solace and strength in his renewed religious faith. While he once denounced Buenos Aires for its pitiless materialism and indifference to the individual, he now tries to accept its way of life, although with some reservation.

III *Gálvez Attacks the Perón Regime*

Since Gálvez reflected Argentine history in so many works, it is not surprising that he should portray some aspect of the turbulent Perón era (1946-1955). It was a change of attitude toward Perón that prompted him to write *Tránsito Guzmán,* at the age of seventy-four. He supported or at least tolerated the dictator during most of his rule for reasons similar to those he advanced in defense of Rosas: maintenance of law and order in the face of civil dissension, preservation of Argentine economic sovereignty, and freedom from foreign political intervention. In 1954, when Perón attacked the Church, Gálvez openly broke with the regime, not being able to reconcile this brazen act with his devotion to Catholicism. The historical events depicted in *Tránsito Guzmán* revolve around that fateful night of June 16, 1955, when many temples, parsonages, and other Church properties in the province of Buenos Aires were burned and sacked by government partisans in retaliation for the bombing of the Casa Rosada (the Argentine White House) and other parts of the capital by bands of revolutionists. *Tránsito Guzmán* is thus not a true historical novel, since it does not look back on history and reconstruct it. Rather, it portrays events witnessed directly by the novelist and experienced emotionally by him. The novel is so earnestly written that we wish the fictional plot had more substance and greater interest. Its main defect lies in Gálvez' inappropriately exalted portrayal of the protagonist, who never emerges as a palpable figure. Tránsito Guzmán, a religious woman strongly opposed to the regime, tries to reconcile her solemn devotion to God with her love for a police officer in Perón's special corps. Her suitor finally defects to the rebel cause because of his love for Tránsito, but dies in one of the bombings of the city. And Tránsito succeeds in carrying out the crucifix from the burning Temple of San Francisco and becomes a heroine to the parishioners. Also a hero is the priest Emilio, at one time imprisoned by Perón, who conforts the wounded during the bombings with no thought of personal safety. After Gálvez ends his idealized tale, the reader can register only shock and horror at the senseless violence of the action described and utter a scathing condemnation of the Perón rule.

IV   *A Final Note*

It is clear that Gálvez' place in the development of the Argentine novel is secure and well defined. And his position in the larger story of Hispanic-American literature is no less significant and lasting. In the preceding pages we have traced his career as a novelist and biographer, analyzing and interpreting his works within the framework of Argentine fiction. His best novels have contributed very significantly to the history of the Argentine novel; indeed, Gálvez was most deeply inspired when he felt he was shaping Argentine fiction, or at least furthering its forward movement. Although he is very much the traditional writer as far as technique and style are concerned, his best fiction adds an important dimension to the novel in realism and the psychological portrayal of character. It is unjust and too simple to label Gálvez the last of the nineteenth-century Realistic novelists; he is a better and more interesting novelist than most of the writers that represented realism and naturalism from 1860 to 1900. His narrative technique is surer, his psychological probing deeper, his descriptions more colorful, exact, and forceful. Even to consider him a transition writer bridging the nineteenth and twentieth centuries implies a certain negative criticism, as if he were somehow lagging behind the times. A writer obviously should be judged according to the literary tastes of his era, but in Gálvez' case this involves more than the usual difficulty, since his novels span so many years and his most important ones were published early in his career. He was neither ahead of his time nor behind it; in his best period, 1914-1930, he was entirely in harmony with it.

Gálvez differs as much from a superficial and unsophisticated novelist like Hugo Wast as he does from an intellectual novelist like Eduardo Mallea. Although Gálvez' novels are easily read and understood and simply presented, they are rarely without social, psychological, or historical significance. He makes us feel man's conflicts; he appeals to our senses and to our emotions, rather than to our intellect. In describing the Argentine scene, he is an accurate, sentient observer who examines what he sees with a microscope and then reacts with his heart; he is not the profound writer who assumes a philosophical or intellectual posture when treating human foibles or society's ills.

With a literary production so vast and varied as Gálvez', it is necessary to separate the enduring works from the ephemeral ones in making a final assessment of his career. To answer the question, "Which works will last? " is difficult. Even the most ardent panegyrist would quickly dismiss many works as minor novels that add little to his stature. The statement by Torres-Ríoseco that "of all the novels of Gálvez, only *La maestra normal* will resist the ravages of time" [3] is true in its implication that it is his best and most important novel, but quite extreme in suggesting such a wide gap between that work and the rest of his production. Few will deny that the sensitive portrayal of Raselda and the masterly evocation of provincial life make *La maestra normal* Gálvez' most accomplished work. But in future years he will also be read for the very human portrait of youthful idealism in *El mal metafísico,* and for his portrayal of the woeful but noble protagonists in *Nacha Regules. La sombra del convento,* principally because of its overly sentimental story, is the most dated of Gálvez' better novels, but will still please many readers for its moving depiction of religious and social intolerance in early twentieth-century Córdoba. And it is likely that the cogent theme of emotional alienation in *Hombres en soledad* will be interpreted by each succeeding generation in accord with the social and moral climate of the times. *Miércoles Santo,* even in its naïveté and stark simplicity, is a timeless novel whose message of spiritual faith drawn from the sorrows of sinners is universally appealing. Of his historical novels, the Paraguayan War trilogy clearly stands out and will be enjoyed for its balanced fusion of fact and fiction. Even in the face of fresh breezes from such Argentine authors as Julio Cortázar and Ernesto Sábato, Gálvez will continue to interest those who seek social and psychological novels of things Argentine. Indeed, Argentina found its commentator in Manuel Gálvez.

Notes and References

Chapter One

1. I am indebted to Manuel Gálvez for furnishing me with some of this biographical information through correspondence from 1953 until his death. I am also most grateful to Señora María Elena Gálvez, the author's widow, for sending me a detailed and meticulously prepared chronology of his life, as well as countless pages of critical material on his works.

The novelist's four volumes of memoirs are a mine of information on Gálvez the man and Gálvez the writer, and I have freely drawn from this source. These memoirs are an obviously partial but valuable document that manifests an overly zealous promotion of his literary reputation. In 1944, he published the first volume, *Amigos y maestros de mi juventud, 1900-1910* (*Friends and Teachers of My Youth, 1900-1910*), which covers the story of his life until 1910. The other three volumes appeared from 1961 to 1965, not without the untiring efforts of Sra. Gálvez, who finally interested Hachette in the manuscript after two other publishers temporized through fear of financial loss.

Biographical data may also be found in: Ignacio B. Anzoátegui, *Manuel Gálvez* (Buenos Aires: Ediciones Culturales Argentinas, 1961), pp. 7-40; Jorge Lafforgue and Jorge B. Rivera, "Realismo tradicional: narrativa urbana," in *Capítulo: la historia de la literatura argentina* (Buenos Aires: Centro Editor de América Latina, 1967), Fascículo 37, pp. 873-88: Nicolás Olivari and Lorenzo Stanchina, *Manuel Gálvez: ensayo sobre su obra* (Buenos Aires: Agencia General de Librería y Publicaciones, 1924), pp. 5-28; Alfredo A. Roggiano, "Manuel Gálvez" in *Diccionario de la literatura latinoamericana: Argentina* (Washington, D.C.: Unión Panamericana, 1961), Part II, 292-93; Jefferson Rea Spell, *Contemporary Spanish-American Fiction* (Chapel Hill: Univ. of N. Carolina Press, 1944), pp. 15-21; Arturo Torres-Ríoseco, *Grandes novelistas de la América Latina* (Berkeley: Univ. of California Press, 1943), Vol. II, *Los novelistas de la ciudad*, 137-45.

2. Among them, *En las redes del amor* (*In Love's Entanglements*).

132

Gálvez did not attempt playwriting again until 1924, when he wrote a dramatic version of his novel *Nacha Regules*. In 1927, he wrote *El hombre de los ojos azules* (*The Man With Blue Eyes*), produced in Córdoba but received with little enthusiasm. And in 1943 he published *Calibán*, but it was never produced. A poorly executed play, it is nevertheless significant in revealing Gálvez' justification of force to protect a nation's political sovereignty and traditions.

3. *En el mundo de los seres ficticios*, p. 362.

4. Gálvez urged creative writers to contribute to *Ideas*, among them Amado Nervo and Roberto Payró.

5. Gálvez wrote on the poetry of Leopoldo Lugones in the June, 1903, issue. He wrote reviews of some thirty-five literary works, among them Benito Pérez Galdós' *La de San Quintín* (May, 1903).

6. *Amigos y maestros de mi juventud*, p. 72.

7. Among them may be cited "Posibilidades del escritor católico" ("Possibilities for the Catholic Writer"), Dec., 1930

8. Examples: "Blasco Ibáñez y su literatura" ("Blasco Ibáñez and His Literature"), March 15, 1928; and "La verdad sobre Sarmiento" ("The Truth About Sarmiento"), May 24, 1928.

9. Anzoátegui, *Manuel Gálvez*, p. 26.

10. Among them "La tristeza de los argentinos" ("The Sadness of Argentines"), Jan., 1930.

11. Examples: "El trágico error de Mussolini" ("Mussolini's Tragic Error"), April 30, 1944; and "Sobre un homenaje a Rosas" ("On a Homage to Rosas"), April 16, 1944.

12. *En el mundo de los seres ficticios*, p. 11. See also Esther H. Turner, "Hispanism in the Life and Works of Manuel Gálvez," unpublished Ph.D. dissertation, Univ. of Washington, 1959.

13. Gálvez translated five stories from five Greek writers, all published in *La Nación*. Example: Thrassos Kastanakis, "El ciego Juan" ("Blind John"), Nov. 21, 1937.

14. Luis Gorosito Heredia, "Nuestros escritores: Manuel Gálvez," *Histonium*, año 10, no. 109 (June, 1948), 434-35.

15. *Los caballeros de la Cruz* (Madrid: Consejo de Gobierno del Banco de España, 1915), pp. 37-38.

16. *En el mundo de los seres ficticios*, p. 94.

17. *Ibid.*, p. 96.

18. Jaimes Freyre published *Los sueños son vida* (*Dreams Are Life*); Ibarbourou, *Lenguas de diamante* (*Tongues of Diamond*).

19. *Entre la novela y la historia*, p. 84.

20. Gálvez' list: Enrique Banchs, Arturo Capdevila, Leopoldo Díaz, Juan Pablo Echagüe, Baldomero Fernández Moreno, Manuel Gálvez, Carlos Ibarguren, Enrique Larreta, Leopoldo Lugones, Calixto Oyuela, Ricardo Rojas. Echagüe and Fernández Moreno were rejected by the nominating committee. The four additional names selected by the

committee were Atilio Chiappori, Gustavo Franceschi, Alberto Gerchunoff, and Juan B. Terán.

21. *Entre la novela y la historia*, p. 96.

22. Abroad too, in Madrid, Paris, Stockholm, and Oslo, his candidacy received favorable publicity in newspapers and journals. He was particularly pleased that Romain Rolland, the 1915 Nobel laureate, generously promoted his nomination.

23. *En el mundo de los seres reales*, p. 353.

24. From a letter Gálvez sent me on October 10, 1957.

Chapter Two

1. For a comprehensive view of the first sixty years of the Argentine novel, see Myron I. Lichtblau, *The Argentine Novel in the Nineteenth Century* (New York: Hispanic Institute in the United States, 1959).

2. Fernando Alegría, in *Breve historia de la novela hispanoamericana* (Mexico: Ediciones de Andrea, 1959), pp. 107-12, categorizes Gálvez as the novelist who best represents the transition from the nineteenth to the twentieth century. Interestingly, he places him in a chapter on "Naturalistic Realism," which forms the last section of Part I, covering fiction through the nineteenth century. He makes this classification despite the fact that the date of Gálvez' first novel is 1914.

3. For studies of these novelists, see Enrique Anderson Imbert, *Tres novelas de Payró con pícaros en tres miras* (Tucumán, Argentina: Univ. Nacional de Tucumán, 1942); and Theodore Andersson, *Carlos María Ocantos: Argentine Novelist* (New Haven: Yale Univ. Press, 1934).

4. *Novelistas contemporáneos hispanoamericanos* (Boston: D.C. Heath, 1964), p. 1.

5. Like most Latin-American novelists, Gálvez also tried his hand at the short story, but with only partial success. He published two volumes of stories, one in 1920 and the other in 1927, but they form an unimportant part of his literary production.

Chapter Three

1. Buenos Aires: Emecé Editores, 1959, p. 37.

2. *Ibid.*

3. *Ibid.*

4. Alberto Zum Felde, in his *Indice crítico de la literatura hispanoamericana: La narrativa* (México: Editorial Guaranía, 1959), pp. 222-23, feels that Gálvez' simple and natural prose frequently degenerates into a commonplace and lifeless style. for Zum Felde, the basic defect lies in its lack of aesthetic sensitivity, which leads to triteness and triviality of narration.

5. *El novelista y las novelas*, p. 51.

6. Emiliano Díez-Echarri and José María Roca Franquesa, *Historia*

de la literatura española e hispanoamericana (Madrid: Aguilar, 1960), p. 1409.

7. *Holy Wednesday*, translated by Warre B. Wells (London: John Lane The Bodley Head, 1934), pp. 3-4. All subsequent page references in the text are to this translation.

8. *El novelista y las novelas*, p. 10.

9. *Nacha Regules*, translated by Leo Angley (New York: E. P. Dutton & Co., 1922), pp. 31-32. All subsequent page references in the text are to this translation.

10. *Amigos y maestros de mi juventud*, p. 109.

11. *La Argentina en nuestros libros*, pp. 44 and 61. Also, *En el mundo de los seres ficticios*, p. 50.

12. *En el mundo de los seres ficticios*, p. 85.

13. *La Argentina en nuestros libros*, p. 44.

14. *Historia de arrabal*, p. 67.

15. *Los caminos de la muerte*, 6th ed. (Buenos Aires: Editorial Losada, 1957), p. 27. All further references are to this edition.

16. *La sombra del convento*, 5th ed. (Buenos Aires: Editorial Tor, 1949), p. 5. All further references are to this edition.

17. *La pampa y su pasión*, 2nd ed. (Buenos Aires: Editorial Tor, n.d., circa 1940), p. 104. All further references are to this edition.

18. *Historia de arrabal*, p. 12.

19. *Ibid.*, p. 84.

20. *La maestra normal*, 9th ed. (Buenos Aires: Editorial Tor, 1950), p. 46. All subsequent references are to this edition.

21. *La sombra del convento*, p. 104.

22. *El mal metafísico*, 8th ed. (Buenos Aires: Espasa-Calpe Argentina, 1962), pp. 73-74. All subsequent references are to this edition.

23. *Che:* interjection used to call attention. *No hablás una palabra:* You don't say a word. This form replaces the usual *No hablas una palabra.* The subject of hablás is *vos*, used instead of *tú. Seguí negando no más:* Just keep on denying it. Used instead of *Sigue negando no más. Macanudo:* wonderful, great. *Macana:* something absurd; stupid act. *Pucha:* coarse interjection of astonishment, doubt, or denial.

24. *El novelista y las novelas*, p. 77.

25. *"Los caminos de la muerte," La Libertad* (Madrid), Aug. 4, 1928, p. 12.

26. For example, *Nacha Regules* has been translated into eleven languages, *Miércoles Santo* into eight, *Historia de arrabal* into four.

27. Fritz Carsten, *"Nacha Regules," Das Literarische Eco* (Berlin), May 1, 1923, p. 6.

28. R. Stern, "Ein argentinischer Zola," *Berliner Zeitung am Mittag*, July 19, 1923, p. 24.

29. Anton Radó, "Manuel Gálvez." *Pester Lloyd* (Budapest), June 19, 1938, p. 24.

30. "Carta a Manuel Gálvez," *Nosotros,* año 17, no. 169 (1923), 283-84.

31. A copy of this letter, dated Copenhagen, May 29, 1924, was sent to me by Gálvez' widow.

32. A translation of Sinclair's article was published in *Vanguardia,* November 19, 1924. I have been unable to locate the American publication in which it originally appeared, although Sra. Gálvez noted in a document she sent me that it was the *New York American,* Nov. 1924.

33. Valery Larbaud, "Un novelista argentino," *La Nación,* April 9, 1933, p. 17.

34. Unsigned review in *L'Information de Paris,* Aug. 29, 1931, p. 9.

35. Louis Parrot, "Sud Amérique," *Lettres Françaises* (Paris), August 8, 1947, p. 16.

36. Nothing pleased Gálvez more than being compared to eminent writers. See *Entre la novela y la historia,* pp. 45-47, 198.

Chapter Four

1. *Breve historia de la novela hispanoamericana,* p. 110. In emphasizing the importance of environment in Gálvez' novels, Alegría goes so far as to call *La maestra normal* "one of the masterpieces of *costumbrismo* in Hispanic America" (*Ibid.,* p. 109). Julio Cejador y Frauca expresses the same view of *La maestra normal* in his *Historia de la lengua y literatura castellana* (Madrid: Revista de archivos, bibliotecas y museos, 1920), Vol XII, 216-17.

2. Jefferson Rea Spell, *Contemporary Spanish-American Fiction,* p. 61.

3. *En el mundo de los seres ficticios,* p. 10.

4. Otis H. Green, "Manuel Gálvez, *Gabriel Quiroga* and *La maestra normal,*" *Hispanic Review,* XI, no. 3 (1943), 240-41.

5. Hugo D. Barbagelata, *La novela y el cuento en Hispanoamérica* (Montevideo: Enrique Miguez, 1947), p. 90.

6. "La plaga del normalismo," *La Nación* (June 8, 1915), p. 14.

7. Leopoldo Lugones, "Por la verdad y la justicia," *La Nación* (June 13, 1915), p. 21.

8. *En el mundo de los seres ficticios,* p. 61.

9. See Alfred Coester, "Manuel Gálvez, Argentine Novelist," *Hispania,* V, no. 6 (1922), 326; and Carmelo M. Bonet, "La novela," in *Historia de la literatura argentina,* ed. Rafael Alberto Arrieta (Buenos Aires: Ediciones Peuser, 1959), IV, 261-62.

10. Enrique Anderson Imbert, in *Historia de la literatura hispanoamericana* (Mexico: Fondo de Cultura Económica, 1954), I, 429, states

that Gálvez describes Carlos Rigas' aesthetic idealism rather listlessly, without spirit or enthusiasm.

11. Nicolás Olivari and Lorenzo Stanchina, *Manuel Gálvez: ensayo sobre su obra* (Buenos Aires: Agencia General de Librería y Publicaciones, 1924), p. 70, see in the abundance of characters a reflection of nineteenth-century European realism.

12. For most critics, Gálvez succeeded well in making the novel a *roman à clef.* A few critics, however, considered this device a major weakness of the work. Julio Noé, in *"El mal metafísico," Nosotros,* año X, no. 83 (1961), 395-97, states that the novel overwhelms the reader with too much environment without synthesis or selectivity. Carlos Alberto Leumann, in *"El mal metafísico," La Nota,* año 2, no. 56 (Sept. 2, 1916), 1105-7, criticizes Gálvez for utilizing real people in an unimaginative and too photographic a fashion, without bothering to convert them into fictional beings with independent personalities.

13. This device of utilizing a character in more than one novel serves to create a greater sense of reality and to provide a kind of unity or common ground between two otherwise independent works. Besides the examples mentioned, there are several other people who appear in two novels: Eduardo Iturbide, in *El mal metafísico* and *La tragedia de un hombre fuerte;* Gervasio Claraval, in *Hombres en soledad* and *El uno y la multitud;* Asunción Belderrain, in *La sombra del convento* and *La tragedia de un hombre fuerte;* and Pedro Roig, in *Hombres en soledad* and *Las dos vidas del pobre Napoleón.*

14. *Contemporary Spanish-American Fiction,* p. 63.

15. Otis H. Green, in "Manuel Gálvez, *Gabriel Quiroga,* and *El mal metafísico," Hispanic Review,* XI, no. 4 (1943), 314-18, points out that one of the basic problems considered in *El mal metafísico*—the appropriate literary expression of the genuine national spirit—was already set forth in *El diario de Gabriel Quiroga,* pp. 182-90.

16. Otis H. Green, *"La sombra del convento* and its Relations to *El diario de Gabriel Quiroga," Hispanic Review,* XII, no. 3 (1944), 196.

17. *En el mundo de los seres ficticios,* p. 101.

18. The Argentine Roberto Giusti, in *"La sombra del convento," Nosotros,* año XI, no. 104 (1917), 517-27, was one of the few who reacted less than enthusiastically to the novel when it first appeared. He criticizes what to him is the rather pedestrian conflict that forms the nucleus of the external action.

19. *Historia de la literatura española e hispanoamericana,* p. 1408.

20. For example, German García, *La novela argentina: un itinerario* (Buenos Aires: Editorial Sudamericana, 1952), p. 120.

Chapter Five

1. Over 105,000 copies have been sold in ten editions, an extraordinary figure for a Latin-American novel.

2. What most attracted many critics to *Nacha Regules* was no doubt its social implications. In the *New York Times Book Review* (April 1, 1923), p. 18, the reviewer states that "the cry and appeal for social pity in *Nacha Regules* have a very interesting similarity to the treatment of Sonya in *Crime and Punishment*."

3. *Contemporary Spanish-American Fiction*, p. 35.

4. *Breve historia de la novela hispanoamericana*, p. 108.

5. Kenneth Fuessle, in his review in the *New York Tribune* (June 10, 1923), p. 23, sees the protagonists' intense search for each other on several occasions throughout the novel as one of the notable achievements of the work.

6. *En el mundo de los seres ficticios*, p. 126. Gálvez' concept of what constitutes a Naturalistic novel was at times arbitrary. In the prologue to *La tragedia de un hombre fuerte*, pp. 8-9, he refuted, in anticipation, those critics who might label it so. He affirmed that his only Naturalistic work was *La maestra normal*, but then added that it did not fall entirely within that category since it contained an element of subjectivity. *El mal metafísico* was in no way Naturalistic, he continued, since the environment did not control the destiny of the characters. Most strangely, Gálvez recognized *Nacha Regules* as a Romantic novel because of its passion and sentiment, placing it on the opposite end of the scale from naturalism and realism.

7. When the English translation appeared in 1923, some American reviewers pointed out that Gálvez handled the theme of vice and prostitution in the most discreet, inoffensive way possible, with scarcely an allusion to sexual matters or smutty material. See, for example, Thomas S. Rice, *"Nacha Regules,"* *Brooklyn Eagle* (May 6, 1923), p. 28.

8. In *Amigos y maestros de mi juventud*, p. 152, Gálvez states that his two-act play *La hija de Antenor*, written in 1902, served as the basis for *Historia de arrabal*.

9. For a study of the socio-religious implications of the Nacha-Monsalvat-Arnedo and the Raselda-Forti-El Chino relationships, see Noé Jitrik, "Los desplazamientos de la culpa en las obras sociales de Manuel Gálvez," *Duquesne Hispanic Review*, II, no. 1 (Spring, 1963), 152-55.

10. Many critics place this novel among Gálvez' best works as regards novelistic technique and emotive power. A few fault the novel's sketchiness and underdeveloped story line. One severe critic, Julio Noé, in *"Historia de arrabal,"* *Nosotros*, año XVII, no. 164 (1923), 127-28, writes that the basic ingredients of the novel seem to be made up of discarded material not used in *Nacha Regules*.

11. Eduardo Barrios, *"La tragedia de un hombre fuerte,"* *La Semana*, Santiago de Chile (Sept. 8, 1922), p. 12.

12. Gálvez' female characters are singled out for analysis in Mireya

Jaimes Freyre, "Gálvez y su laberinto," *Revista Iberoamericana*, XVIII, no. 36 (1953), 317-30; and in Leonard E. Stevens, "Feminine Protagonists in Manuel Gálvez' Novels," unpublished Ph.D. dissertation, Indiana Univ., 1964.

13. *La novela argentina*, p. 123.

14. "Manuel Gálvez, Argentine novelist," *Hispania*, V, no. 3 (1922), 327.

15. Elena Carrero del Mármol, "Galvez y Mallea: Imágenes de la Argentina," *Duquesne Hispanic Review*, II, no. 1 (Spring, 1963), 172.

16. *En el mundo de los seres ficticios*, p. 267.

17. Coester, "Manuel Gálvez: Argentine Novelist," p. 327.

18. When Gálvez was writing *Hombres en soledad*, he stated that the novel would be disjointed and lack a conventional plot, each character merely playing out his own inner drama. See M. Rodríguez Luján, "Manuel Gálvez ha escrito una novela sobre la soledad en Buenos Aires," *El Hogar*, Buenos Aires, año 32, no. 1412 (Nov. 6, 1936), p. 10.

19. Gálvez is very much aware of his early treatment of this theme in Argentine fiction, especially his antedating Eduardo Mallea. In *En el mundo de los seres ficticios*, p. 196, Gálvez points out that as early as 1920 he published a story dealing with the emotional solitude of a young pianist: "Historia de un momento espiritual" ("Story of a Spiritual Moment").

20. Manuel Pedro González, in *"Hombres en soledad* de Manuel Gálvez," *Revista Iberoamericana*, II, no. 4 (1940), 423, states that Claraval's plight fails to move the reader because he himself and not his social environment is essentially at fault.

21. *Hombres en soledad*, 2nd ed. (Buenos Aires: Editorial Losada, 1942), pp. 131-32. All further references are to this edition.

22. "La soledad de los espíritus en la Argentina," *France-Amérique-Latine*, Paris, XXIX, no. 323 (Nov. 1938), 321.

23. *The Bay of Silence*, translated by Stuart Edgar Grummon (New York: Alfred A. Knopf, 1944), p. 339.

24. See, for example, Arturo Torres-Ríoseco, *Grandes novelistas de la América Hispana*, II, 147; and Juan B. González, *"La pampa y su pasión," Nosotros*, año XXI, no. 212 (1927), 115.

25. Reference is to the second edition (Buenos Aires: Editorial Tor, n.d., circa 1940), p. 190.

Chapter Six

1. *Entre la novela y la historia*, p. 40.

2. In *"Jornadas de agonía* y la técnica de Gálvez," *Nosotros*, año XXIV, no. 248 (1930), 126, Ramón Doll criticizes Gálvez for applying the same novelistic formula to all his novels, for insisting that there is a set of fixed rules and procedures to follow for all types of fiction.

3. For an account of the action in the three novels, see Henry A.

Holmes, "Una trilogía de Manuel Gálvez: *Escenas de la Guerra del Paraguay," Revista Hispánica Moderna,* III, no. 3 (1937), 201-12.

4. See, for example, Georges Pillement, "Manuel Gálvez et le roman argentin moderne," *La Revue Européenne,* Paris (Oct., 1930), p. 12. The Spaniard E. Gómez de Baquero, in "Un episodio nacional argentino," *El Sol,* Madrid (May 30, 1928), p. 21, suggests that the trilogy may be compared to Galdós' *Episodios nacionales.*

5. Yet some critics feel that by overloading the novels with too much unimportant detail Gálvez attenuated the force of the narrative. See, for example, Guillermo Cotto-Thorner, "Manuel Gálvez y su trilogía de la guerra paraguaya," *Revista Iberoamericana,* XVI, no. 31 (1950), 87.

6. *Los caminos de la muerte,* 6th ed. (Buenos Aires: Editorial Losada, 1957), p. 111. Further references are to this edition.

7. The French paid Gálvez high tribute when in 1939 the Naval Academy selected *Los caminos de la muerte* as one of the required books for aspiring officers.

8. *"Los caminos de la muerte," Criterio,* Buenos Aires, año IX, no. 13 (May 31, 1928), 409.

9. *Humaitá,* 3rd. ed. (Buenos Aires: Editorial Tor, n.d., circa 1932-1935), pp. 55-56. Further references are to this edition.

10. For a few critics, Gálvez' treatment of the historical figures, such as General Mitre, is limp and stilted. See, for example, José Bianco, *"Los caminos de la muerte," Nosotros,* año XXII, no. 230 (1928), 101.

11. In "Gálvez y la novela histórica: el ciclo Rosista," *Duquesne Hispanic Review,* II, no. 1 (Spring 1963), 183-84, Norma Desinano states that many historical personages in the Rosas novels are more vividly revealed than the fictional creations and become the true protagonists.

12. *En el mundo de los seres reales,* p. 200.

13. An Argentine film based on the novel appeared in 1953, produced by Leo Fleider.

Chapter Seven

1. In *Entre la novela y la historia,* p. 170, Gálvez offers circumstantial reasons for having entered biography in the 30's. He states that that genre was very much in vogue and perhaps threatening to dislodge the novel, as could be seen by the success of André Maurois' *Disraeli* (1927) and Stefan Zweig's *Joseph Fouché* (1930). Furthermore, Gálvez writes, it was becoming increasingly difficult to convince editorial houses to publish novels when so few people were reading them.

2. Tomás de Lara, "Medio siglo de novela argentina visto en seis primorosas ediciones españolas," *Argentina,* año 1, no. 7 (Aug. 1, 1949), 56, after stating that Gálvez' *Hombres en soledad* and *Escenas*

de la Guerra del Paraguay are high points in Latin-American fiction, adds that he should have continued exclusively with the novel and not have entered biography.

3. Manuel P. González, "El Yrigoyen de Manuel Gálvez," *Revista Hispánica Moderna,* año 9, no. 4 (1943), 314, aptly calls the work a "psychobiography or spiritual biography."

4. *Biografías completas* (Buenos Aires: Emecé Editores, 1962), I, 20-21. All subsequent textual references to Gálvez' biographical works are to the two-volume *Biografías completas.*

5. Gálvez' defense of force and tyranny is also seen in *Vida de don Gabriel García Moreno,* 1941. The Ecuadorian dictator's concordat with Pope Pius IX and his attempt to make his country a Catholic utopia endeared him to Gálvez despite the oppressive measures adopted to achieve his goals. Gálvez' last biography of celebrated political figures, *Don Francisco de Miranda,* 1947, extols the life of the great precursor of Latin-American independence.

Three minor works complete Gálvez' efforts in biography. *Vida de Aparicio Saravia,* 1942, treats of a famed gaucho *caudillo* who represents for Gálvez the quintessence of the Uruguayan spirit. *José Hernández,* 1945, is a literary biography of the author of the epic gaucho poem *Martín Fierro. El santito de la toldería (The Young Saint of the Indian Camp),* 1947, is a simple, pleasant book that relates the life of one Ceferino Namuncurá, who reached Christian perfection within the confines of his indigenous heritage.

Chapter Eight

1. "A Priest's Struggle," unsigned review in the *New York Times Book Review,* July 22, 1934, p. 14.

2. *Entre la novela y la historia,* p. 236.

3. *La locura de ser santo* depicts the qualities of supreme saintliness and altruism in the thoughts and deeds of a young teacher.

4. Donald F. Brown, "An Argentine 'Doña Perfecta': Galdós and Manuel Gálvez," *Hispania,* XLVII, no. 2 (1964), 282-87, makes a comparison between Teodoro's mother and the religiously bigoted matriarch of the famous Spanish novel (1876) that bears her name.

Chapter Nine

1. At his death in 1962, Gálvez left behind many unedited manuscripts he had written in various periods in his long career. To date, only the novel *La locura de ser santo* has been published, but Gálvez' widow is actively engaged in trying to interest publishers in the remaining works. I have not had access to any of these, but Señora Gálvez, who has read all the manuscripts, indicated in a letter to me, dated November 25, 1963, that the most important is *La gran familia*

de los Laris (*The Great Laris Family*). Unlike any other of Gálvez' works, this novel "presents a sweeping view of Argentina across three generations, from 1905 to 1955, and contains the evolution of customs and material on politics and immigration." H. Ernest Lewald has assembled Señora Gálvez' comments on her husband's unedited works in an informative note: "Libros inéditos de Manuel Gálvez," *Hispania*, LII, no. 4 (1969), 954-55.

2. Thematic similarities and differences in the two novels are examined in Norma Desinano, *La novelística de Manuel Gálvez* (Santa Fe, Argentina: Univ. Nacional del Litoral, 1965), pp. 38-47.

3. *Grandes novelistas de la América Hispana*, II, 156.

Selected Bibliography

PRIMARY SOURCES

The Writings of Manuel Gálvez

The first edition of each work is listed. When I have not used the first edition, I have indicated in the "Notes and References" the particular edition used. Only books are noted here; articles in newspapers and magazines are omitted.

1. Collections

Obras escogidas (Madrid: Aguilar, 1949). Prologue by Gálvez and transcription of an interview that Juan Carlos Moreno had with the novelist. Contents: *La maestra normal, El mal metafísico, La sombra del convento,* "Luna de miel," *Miércoles Santo, El gaucho de Los Cerrillos,* "Una santa criatura."

Biografías completas (Buenos Aires: Emecé Editores, 1962). Vols. I and II. Prologue by Carmelo Bonet.

2. Fiction

La maestra normal (Buenos Aires: Sociedad Cooperativa Nosotros, 1914).

El mal metafísico (Buenos Aires: Sociedad Cooperativa Nosotros, 1916).

La sombra del convento (Buenos Aires: Sociedad Cooperativa Nosotros, 1917).

Nacha Regules (Buenos Aires: Editorial Pax, 1919). English translation by Leo Angley (New York: E. P. Dutton & Co., 1922).

Luna de miel y otras narraciones (Buenos Aires: Biblioteca de Novelistas Americanos, 1920).

La tragedia de un hombre fuerte (Buenos Aires: Biblioteca de Novelistas Americanos, 1922).

Historia de arrabal (Buenos Aires: Agencia General de Librería y Publicaciones, 1922).

El cántico espiritual (Buenos Aires: Agencia General de Librería y Publicaciones, 1923).

La pampa y su pasión (Buenos Aires: Agencia General de Librería y Publicaciones, 1926).

Una mujer muy moderna (Buenos Aires: Editorial Gleizer, 1927).

Los caminos de la muerte (Buenos Aires: La Facultad, 1928).

Humaitá (Buenos Aires: La Facultad, 1929).

Jornadas de agonía (Buenos Aires: La Facultad, 1929).

Miércoles Santo (Buenos Aires: La Facultad, 1930). English translation by Warre B. Wells (London: John Lane The Bodley Head, Ltd., 1934).

El gaucho de Los Cerrillos (Buenos Aires: La Facultad, 1931).

El General Quiroga (Buenos Aires: La Facultad, 1932).

Cautiverio (Buenos Aires: Sociedad Amigos del Libro Rioplatense, 1935).

La noche toca a su fin (Buenos Aires: Editorial Cabaut, 1935).

Hombres en soledad (Buenos Aires: Club del Libro, 1938).

La ciudad pintada de rojo (Buenos Aires: Instituto Panamericano de Cultura, 1948).

La muerte en las calles (Buenos Aires: El Ateneo, 1949).

Tiempo de odio y angustia (Buenos Aires: Espasa-Calpe Argentina, 1951).

Han tocado a degüello (Buenos Aires: Espasa-Calpe Argentina, 1951).

Bajo la garra anglo-francesa (Buenos Aires: Espasa-Calpe Argentina, 1953).

Y así cayó don Juan Manuel (Buenos Aires: Espasa-Calpe Argentina, 1954).

Las dos vidas del pobre Napoleón (Buenos Aires: Editorial Losada, 1954). For student use there is an edition with notes, exercises, and vocabulary by Myron I. Lichtblau (New York: Charles Scribner's Sons, 1963).

El uno y la multitud (Buenos Aires: Ediciones Alpe, 1955).

Tránsito Guzmán (Buenos Aires: Ediciones Theoría, 1956).

Perdido en su noche (Buenos Aires: Editorial Sudamericana, 1958).

Me mataron entre todos (Buenos Aires: Emecé Editores, 1962).

La locura de ser santo (Buenos Aires: Ediciones Puma, 1967).

3. Poetry

El enigma interior (Buenos Aires: Private Edition, 1907).

El sendero de humildad (Buenos Aires: A. Moen, 1909).

Poemas para la recién llegada (Buenos Aires: Ediciones Theoría, 1957).

4. Drama

Nacha Regules (Buenos Aires: Agencia General de Librería y Publicaciones, 1924).

El hombre de los ojos azules (Buenos Aires: La Facultad, 1928).
Calibán (Buenos Aires: Private Edition, 1943).

5. Biography

Vida de Fray Mamerto Esquiú (Buenos Aires: Editorial Tor, 1933).
Vida de Hipólito Yrigoyen (Buenos Aires: Editorial Tor, 1939).
Vida de don Juan Manuel de Rosas (Buenos Aires: El Ateneo, 1940).
Vida de don Gabriel García Moreno (Buenos Aires: Editorial Difusión, 1942).
Vida de Aparicio Saravia (Buenos Aires: Private Edition, 1942).
Vida de Sarmiento (Buenos Aires: Emecé Editores, 1945).
José Hernández (Buenos Aires: La Universidad, 1945).
Don Francisco de Miranda (Buenos Aires: Emecé Editores, 1947).
El santito de la toldería (Buenos Aires: Poblet, 1947).

6. Essays

El diario de Gabriel Quiroga (Buenos Aires: A. Moen, 1910).
El solar de la raza (Buenos Aires: Sociedad Cooperativa Nosotros, 1913).
La inseguridad de la vida obrera (Buenos Aires: Alsina, 1913).
La vida múltiple (Buenos Aires: Sociedad Cooperativa Nosotros, 1916).
El espíritu de aristocracia y otros ensayos (Buenos Aires: Agencia General de Librería y Publicaciones, 1924).
Este pueblo necesita (Buenos Aires: A. García Santos, 1934).
La Argentina en nuestros libros (Santiago de Chile: Editorial Ercilla, 1935).
España y algunos españoles (Buenos Aires: Editorial Huarpes, 1945).
El novelista y las novelas (Buenos Aires: Emecé Editores, 1949).

7. Memoirs

The following four volumes comprise *Recuerdos de la vida literaria:*

Amigos y maestros de mi juventud, 1900-1910 (Buenos Aires: Kraft, 1944).
En el mundo de los seres ficticios (Buenos Aires: Hachette, 1961).
Entre la novela y la historia (Buenos Aires: Hachette, 1962).
En el mundo de los seres reales (Buenos Aires: Hachette, 1965).

8. Translation

With Roberto F. Giusti. Romain Rolland, *Clerambault* (Buenos Aires: Editorial Pax, 1921).

SECONDARY SOURCES

The most complete bibliography of Manuel Gálvez was compiled by Natalio Kisnerman for the very valuable series *Bibliografía Argentina de Artes y Letras* (Buenos Aires: Fondo Nacional de Las Artes, 1964). Other useful bibliographies are included in Olivari and Stanchina's *Manuel Gálvez: ensayo sobre su obra;* and in *Diccionario de la literatura latinoamericana.* For additional titles, particularly the most recent ones, the reader should consult the annual bibliography in the *Publications of the Modern Language Association* and *The Year's Work in Romance Languages and Literatures.*

Only the most important items cited in "Notes and References" are repeated here.

1. Books and Monographs

ANZOÁTEGUI, IGNACIO B. *Manuel Gálvez* (Buenos Aires: Ediciones Culturales Argentinas, 1961). Very limited in scope and in critical appraisal, but contains some interesting biographical details and miscellaneous information on several works.

DESINANO, NORMA. *La novelística de Manuel Gálvez* (Santa Fe, Argentina: Universidad Nacional del Litoral, 1965). Broad commentary and impartial criticism of Gálvez' most important novels. Solid appraisal, in particular, of *Hombres en soledad.*

OLIVARI, NICOLAS and STANCHINA, LORENZO. *Manuel Gálvez: ensayo sobre su obra* (Buenos Aires: Agencia General de Librería y Publicaciones, 1924). Completely favorable, straightforward, lucid account of Gálvez' early writings, including his poetry, essays, and short stories, as well as his novels. Study at times lacks objectivity and qualitative evaluation.

2. Articles

By way of explanation, it should be pointed out that Ricardo Rojas' monumental eight-volume *Historia de la literatura argentina,* which appeared between 1917 and 1925, contains just a few scattered references to Gálvez since the work excluded living writers.

ALEGRÍA, FERNANDO. "Manuel Gálvez," in *Breve historia de la novela hispanoamericana* (Mexico: Ediciones de Andrea, 1959), pp. 107-12. Fine synthesis of the salient characteristics of Gálvez' novelistic technique. Only two novels are singled out for special analysis.

BARBAGELATA, HUGO, "Manuel Gálvez," in *La novela y el cuento en Hispanoamérica* (Montevideo: Enrique Miguez, 1947), pp. 89-97. Enthusiastic survey of his fiction.

BONET, CARMELO. "La novela," in *Historia de la literatura argentina,* ed. Rafael A. Arrieta (Buenos Aires: Editorial Peuser, 1959), IV, 260-69. Sketchy, rather unsubstantial presentation of Gálvez' fiction and its importance in the development of the Argentine novel.

BROWN, DONALD F. "The Catholic Naturalism of Manuel Gálvez," *Modern Language Quarterly*, IX, no. 2 (1948), 165-76. Mature, well-documented study, showing how Gálvez reconciles in his novels Christian belief in free will and deterministic naturalism.

CARRERO DEL MÁRMOL, ELENA. "Gálvez y Mallea: Imágenes de la Argentina," *Duquesne Hispanic Review*, II, no. 1 (1963), 167-78.

CHAPMAN, ARNOLD. "Manuel Gálvez y Eduardo Mallea," *Revista Iberoamericana*, XIX, no. 37 (1953), 71-78. Well-researched, scholarly article showing points of contact and fundamental differences in themes and psychological penetration in the two novelists.

CRAWFORD, WILLIAM REX. *A Century of Latin-American Thought* (Cambridge: Harvard University Press, 1961), pp. 149-64. Magnifying Gálvez' role in shaping modern Argentine thought, Crawford discusses his idealism and nationalism as professed in his essays.

DÍEZ-ECHARRI, EMILIANO and ROCA FRANQUESA, JOSÉ MARÍA "Manuel Gálvez," in *Historia de la literatura española e hispanoamericana* (Madrid: Aguilar, 1960), pp. 1406-9. A useful survey of Gálvez' fiction, grouped as social novels, psychological novels, and historical novels.

GIUSTI, ROBERTO F. *"La sombra del convento,"* *Nosotros*, año 11, no. 104(1917), 517-27. The author of the article is not convinced of the verisimilitude of Gálvez' works or of his technical skill as a novelist.

GONZÁLEZ, MANUEL P. *"Hombres en soledad* de Manuel Gálvez," *Revista Iberoamericana*, II, no. 4 (1940), 419-25. Criticizes Gálvez for painting such an unfavorable picture of Buenos Aires and for creating such needlessly pessimistic and despairing characters.

GREEN, OTIS H. "Manuel Gálvez, *Gabriel Quiroga* and *La maestra normal,"* *Hispanic Review*, XI, no. 3 (1943), 221-52. Excellent thematic study of the relationship between Gálvez' early essays and his first novel.

————— *"La sombra del convento* and its relations to *El diario de Gabriel Quiroga,"* *Hispanic Review*, XII, no. 3 (1944), 196-210. A good account of the evolution of Gálvez' religious thinking from essay to fiction.

JAIMES FREYRE, MIREYA. "Gálvez y su laberinto," *Revista Iberoamericana*, XVIII, no. 36 (1953), 315-37. Examines the special qualities of Gálvez' objective realism, character portrayal, and psychological insights.

JITRIK, NOÉ. "Los desplazamientos de la culpa en las obras sociales de Manuel Gálvez," *Duquesne Hispanic Review*, II, no. 1 (1963), 143-66. Solid critical analysis of motivational forces and psychological meanings in selected novels.

LAFFORGUE, JORGE and RIVERA, JORGE B. "Realismo tradicional: narrativa urbana," in *Capítulo: la historia de la literatura argentina* (Buenos Aires: Centro Editor de América Latina, 1967), Fascículo 37, pp. 873-88. Loosely presented, journalistic survey of Gálvez' career, but valuable for making the novelist a very live figure in the literary world of Argentina.

LEUMANN, CARLOS ALBERTO. *"El mal metafísico,"* La nota, año 2, no. 56 (Sept. 2, 1916), 1105-7. A scathing criticism of the novel.

NOÉ, JULIO. *"El mal metafísico,"* Nosotros, año X, no. 83 (1916), 393-400. One of the most reasoned of the early reviews; points out the aesthetic limitations of Gálvez' exact realism.

ROGGIANO, ALFREDO. "Manuel Gálvez," in *Diccionario de la literatura latinoamericana. Argentina* (Washington, D.C.: Unión Panamericana, 1961), II, 292-98. Very good overall view of the evolution of Gálvez' writings.

SPELL, JEFFERSON REA. "City Life in the Argentine as Seen by Manuel Gálvez," in *Contemporary Spanish-American Fiction* (Chapel Hill: Univ. of North Carolina Press, 1944), pp. 15-63. The first major account in English of Gálvez' fiction. Detailed plot summaries as well as intelligent critical commentary.

TORRES-RÍOSECO, ARTURO. "Manuel Gálvez," in *Grandes novelistas de la América Hispana* (Berkeley: Univ. of California Press, 1943), II, 137-60. Comprehensive, perceptive view of Gálvez' principal novels. Commentaries are highly original, if at times too subjective.

ZUM FELDE, ALBERTO. "Manuel Gálvez," in *Indice crítico de la literatura hispanoamericana: La narrativa* (Mexico: Editorial Guaranía, 1959), pp. 217-25. Favorable and very unfavorable comments are mixed with unusually keen literary acumen.

Index

84687

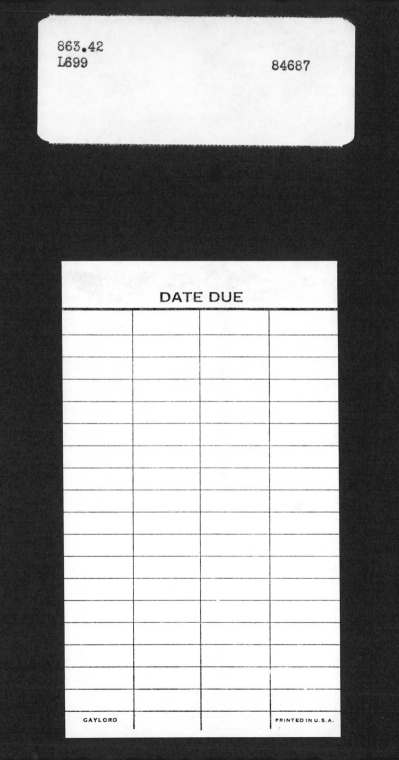

DATE DUE

GAYLORD			PRINTED IN U.S.A.